PRAISE FOR WONDER WOMEN

"It is a real pity Katy and Giles didn't write this book a few years ago. Companies today would be more creative, open-minded and versatile."

Javier Sánchez Lamelas, Author of *MARTKeting: The heart and the brain of branding*, and founder & CEO, Top Line Marketing Consulting

"A wonderful celebration of the experiences and successes of some inspirational women in the marketing industry. I've no doubt that profiling their impact will help inspire the next generation, as well as those who are in the throes of their career right now."

Emma Isaac, Marketing Week Top 100 Most Effective Marketers 2020, Member of WACL

"Marketing is a comparatively young business discipline but if you want to understand why women are now shaping how best practice is evolving, take a look at *Wonder Women*. Giles and Katy's book is a bumper bundle of inspiration that combines vintage success stories with the up-to-the-minute thoughts of emerging talent."

Paul Walton, The Brand Historian, and founder, Strategic Leaps

"That 'evidence matters' in inspiring change is powerfully illustrated by this wonderful collection of interviews and stories, featuring, quite rightly, two iconic women from the business of evidence!"

Jane Frost CBE, CEO, MRS

"If we needed reminding just how focused, determined, and creative women are at work, then look no further than *Wonder Women*, which tells the stories of some incredible pioneers, past and present. Giles and Katy summarize things perfectly; it is together we thrive, men and women united in coming up with solutions to help each other, in a world which has never needed our collaboration more."

Charlotte Lambkin, Member of UK Advisory Board at Edelman

"*Wonder Women* comes at a perfect time and, in some ways, not nearly soon enough, recounting the amazingly insightful, brave, creative and brilliant manoeuvres women have taken to not only be heard or recognized, but to break through the glass ceiling and shine – and with their contribution – forever change the game. 'Wonder'-fully inspirational read for anyone seeking to stand up and standout."

Hilarie S Viener, Founder, Viener&Partners, and CEO, Genius 100 Foundation

"In a 15-year marketing career, the greatest single piece of information I've learned is that we business folk in our fancy offices are nothing like the people we sell to. Through the stories in *Wonder Women*, Giles and Katy have reminded me why diversity of gender, thought and character is utterly vital to our industry's success. Does gender bias remain in the 'woke' workplace of today? Absolutely. But, with ongoing understanding and recognition of the expertise a varied workforce brings, things will continue to improve. These stories bring enjoyable heft, as well as evidence to support the progress being made."

Will Butterworth, Director, Edelman

Published by
LID Publishing Limited
The Record Hall, Studio 304,
16-16a Baldwins Gardens,
London EC1N 7RJ, UK

info@lidpublishing.com
www.lidpublishing.com

A member of:

BPR
Business Publishers Roundtable

www.businesspublishersroundtable.com

Printed by CPI Group (UK) Ltd, Croydon CR0 4YY
ISBN: 978-1-912555-87-1
ISBN: 978-1-911671-23-7 (ebook)

Cover design: Matthew Renaudin
Page design: Caroline Li

W⚲NDER W⚲MEN

INSPIRING STORIES & INSIGHTFUL INTERVIEWS WITH WOMEN IN MARKETING

GILES LURY
KATY MOUSINHO

MADRID | MEXICO CITY | LONDON
NEW YORK | BUENOS AIRES
BOGOTA | SHANGHAI | NEW DELHI

CONTENTS

A WOMAN'S PLACE

A WOMAN'S WORK

INSIGHTFUL INTERVIEWS
19 INTERVIEWS WITH SUCCESSFUL WOMEN
IN MARKETING

1970s–1980s: WOMEN'S LIB

1990s–2000s: GIRL POWER

FOREWORD

BY EDWINA DUNN, OBE

Edwina is a data science entrepreneur who has always been fascinated by people's stories and motivations. As the co-founder of worldwide loyalty programmes such as Tesco's Clubcard, Edwina knows first-hand what it feels like to work in a male-dominated industry, and how women's lack of confidence so often holds them back.

Edwina created 'The Female Lead' to be a platform that celebrates women's stories and showcases the lesser-known successes of women in order to support and encourage the next generation.

This is a book that I think is important.

We are at a tipping point in the way society sees, treats and values women, but there is still much more to be done. Despite huge advances, gender inequality remains a fact throughout the world, affecting social, political and economic life. Women are paid less, underrepresented in government and media, and are often still financially dependent on men. This impacts the economic output of the United Kingdom and indeed the world. By better harnessing women's skills, the social and economic benefits would be huge.

Research shows that an absence of accessible, inspirational role models is a barrier to developing successful, ambitious women.

Organizations like The Female Lead, which I helped found, are dedicated to offering alternative role models to those presented by popular culture and celebrating women's achievements across a wide and diverse range of sectors and roles.

The Female Lead creates a variety of spaces for women to present themselves, including a book of 60 amazing women from around the world (February 2017), an online and social media presence, and an outreach programme for girls in schools, celebrating female role models who shape the world.

We know from our work in schools that young women today still feel that there is a lack of diverse women to look up to in popular culture.

The key difference with this book is that *Wonder Women*, while sharing some of our aims, focuses on only one industry, and it's one I know well – marketing. This book, therefore, has the space to explore the sector more fully and Katy and Giles bring their wealth of experience and insight to the topic.

I have personal experience of the prejudices and obstacles that can stop or hold back women in marketing and have related how, together with my partner Clive Humby, I overcame them. I'm proud that my story features among the others showcased in this book.

Like the authors, I think the current marketing industry role models are too biased toward men, and I applaud their drive to change that.

I think the choice of structure is perceptive, too; the combination of stories and interviews is about engaging the reader, not force-feeding them. It is a more emotional approach than a textbook or many business books. Some might say it is a more 'feminine' approach.

The stories have a lightness of touch and introduced me to many people, brands and incidents I didn't know.

The strength, insights and drive of the women featured in the stories is amazing, and there are lessons we can all draw from them.

The interviews allowed me to get a feel for some of the other Wonder Women, hearing their voices. It is an approach we have used widely at The Female Lead. Again, I have met and know some of the interviewees but there were many who are new to me and several I would love to meet.

Together, the stories and the interviews help provide a rich list of diverse role models that the next generation of marketers, both women and men, can look up to, learn from and aspire to emulate.

The concluding section draws insights from the stories, the interviews and from the extensive research Katy and Giles have obviously done, but it maintains a more conversational tone rather than a heavy academic one. The points are still well made and very pertinent.

Finally, I couldn't agree more with the authors' conclusion about the brave new world where successful marketing will be driven by a diversity of thinking. As my own career demonstrates, it's not about men or women, and it's not about masculine or feminine traits, it's about what I would call, 'The Power of Two' – my leadership model that I started at dunnhumby 20 years ago – and have taken to my new company, Starcount. It combines two people with opposite skills, male or female, to lead together so they can complement each other. When this happens, anything is possible. 1+1 can equal 3, which is an interesting thought for a data scientist.

Edwina Dunn OBE
25 March 2020

3

INTRODUCTION

The inspiration

Every marketer knows the stories of Lord Lever, Charles Revson and Steve Jobs, has probably read Al Ries and Jack Trout, Philip Kotler and Byron Sharp and seen the work of Bill Bernbach, David Ogilvy, Wally Olins and John Hegarty. What's interesting about these 'Masters of Marketing' is that they are all MEN.

The huge contribution to marketing by women – the innovations, the creation of brands, their design, their growth and their often amazing revitalizations – is, by contrast, often ignored or overlooked. Their stories, their challenges and their successes just don't get the same airtime.

Giles Lury is a brilliant brand storyteller, but when he looked back over the 250 stories he has published in his books *The Prisoner and the Penguin, How Coca-Cola Took Over the World* and *Inspiring Innovation*, he was shocked to discover that in only 15% of them the lead protagonist was a woman.

So, he decided to right the wrong and write a book dedicated to these 'Wonder Women' – the women who invented, nurtured, built and rebuilt the brands we know and love today.

Katy Mousinho came on board because promoting the unique talents, energy and intellect of women in business and at home is a cause she's passionate about. Giles and many others might well recommend her as a candidate for Wonder Women herself. She has had a highly successful career, including Managing Director at Hauck Research International and The Value Engineers. She is a successful insight specialist, a trainer in personal development and an inspiration and role model for many she has worked with.

What we hope to achieve with the book

One of our interviewees turned the table on us and, before agreeing to participate, she asked us to set out what we wanted to achieve with the book. It was a good question and certainly deserves an answer.

We can honestly say that our aims are about and for the industry we have both spent our working lives in. Sales of the book would be nice. Some praise and recognition are always welcome. But neither of those are our main drivers.

After a little discussion, we agreed on three objectives:

1. To create awareness of and celebrate women's success in the world of marketing.
2. To inspire others (both women and men) with the stories and thoughts of successful women and encourage marketers to adopt what we believe are the more 'feminine' aspects of thinking and doing.
3. To encourage all women in marketing to recognize, have confidence in and grow their talents.

We want to achieve balance in the book. We didn't want the book to be too strident: this isn't a book that 'bashes' men. It does, however, champion women and changes the narrative around the feminine traits that are too often characterized negatively.

Why the time is right for this book

Not only do we have enough miles on the clock and enough experience to feel able to write this book, we believe that a number of factors and trends are aligning so that people are likely to be more open to the messages that we want to get across.

We think we're at an exciting tipping point.

Feminism is all too often a contentious word, but when you ask people how they feel about women and men being equal, most claim to be in favour. After winning the right to vote in the first wave, feminists have been fighting for liberation, individualism, and equal opportunities for themselves and others ever since. We're now in the fourth wave of feminism, where the internet and social media have enabled diverse voices to be heard.

In October 2017, this was brought into sharp focus as the #MeToo movement began to spread virally and hit the headlines. This gave all women the voice to speak out, certainly against harassment, but also about a host of other injustices, including equal opportunities in the workplace and the gender pay gap.

As a result, we are beginning to hear women's voices more and see more women in leading roles in parliament, business, television, film, sport and social media. Amazing women in history are also emerging, and some amazing female role models are at last coming into the spotlight.

Further reassessment of the respective roles of men and women is being seen in:

- Changes in technology that are reshaping how and where people work, with more opportunities for flexible hours and working from home. The enforced changes that occurred during the COVID-19 crisis may actually help speed this process up as organizations have seen that much can be achieved while working from home, with more flexible hours and greater use of videoconferencing.

- The latest thinking in management and leadership moving on from the more hierarchical structures and command-and-control approaches to flatter management teams and more collaboration and interdependence.

- The positive reassessment of certain traits historically ascribed to women and often belittled. Intuition is just one example, where the old negative term of 'a woman's intuition' has been challenged by books like *Blink* by Malcolm Gladwell and a new interpretation as superfast superlogic is increasingly accepted.

Has anger become a force for good?

Throughout history, and as highlighted in some of our interviews, women have often adopted an attitude of 'just ignore and carry on' and don't make a fuss. However, in recent times there has been a release of all that stored anger, channelling it to good effect.

In many ways, this isn't seen as a feminine trait but can serve women well, as the suffragettes proved. Nowadays, you have role models like Cindy Gallop Niño, who is the central character in one of our stories but gave the following advice at the Creative Equals' Future Leaders conference in London in May 2018: "Forget passion; find something you want to punch." Audre Lorde's *The Uses of Anger: Women responding to racism* tells us, "Every woman has a well-stocked arsenal of anger potentially useful against those oppressions, personal and institutional. Focused with precision, it can become a powerful source of energy serving progress and change."

Why the three sections?

At the heart of this book are the stories. Storytelling as a means of emotionally engaging people while getting them to think is something that we have long championed. We have grouped these stories around the themes we identified and will discuss later in the book.

The addition of interviews seems only natural as it allows you, the reader, to get a feel for how some of these successful women talk and get their points across. We are indebted to them for their time, their honesty and their passion, and we believe these interviews have significantly enriched the book.

Finally, 'Insights and Thoughts on a Brave New World' felt like a means of pulling everything we learned together and presenting some of our thoughts on what the future might hold. This probably isn't exhaustive, and we do encourage you to think about the contents and the conclusions you would draw and your hopes and actions for the future.

A note on biases, not absolutes

Everyone we spoke to recognized that the traits and differences between men and women we discussed are not truly universal.

They were very conscious and at times concerned about making sweeping generalizations. We agreed with them that it was therefore important to put in this 'health warning' at the front of the book.

Put simply, the warning is that when we and the interviewees are discussing the differences between men and women, their attitudes and behaviours, they are talking about those that are either generally attributed to the different sex or that they feel are significant differences.

The differences are indicative, not exclusive. We and they know that there are many women who exhibit what are generally accepted as 'masculine' traits like focus, quantitative analysis and drive, and there are many men who exhibit 'feminine' traits like empathy, intuition and team building.

The biases are, however, significant and have an impact on how women are seen, the social pressure they feel, and also the opportunities they are given to perform key roles in marketing for which their skills and talents complement and sometimes exceed (many) men's abilities.

We and all the interviewees would advocate a future not where women dominate, but where diversity is valued and encouraged, and both sexes have equal opportunities to contribute to the success of the brand and the business they work on and for.

Katy Mousinho and Giles Lury
2020

INSPIRING
STORIES

THE STORIES

GIRL POWER

1. The queen of Tupperware
   – Brownie Wise – Tupperware

2. Don't let them grind you down
   – Wendy Gordon – Research Business

3. Not playing the field, levelling it
   – Whitney Wolfe Herd – Bumble (& Tinder)

4. To boldly go where no Barbie has gone before
   – Samantha Critoforetti – ESA and Mattel/Barbie

5. Heads or tails
   – Jean and Jane Ford – Benefit

6. Finding your passion
   – Debbie Sterling – GoldieBlox

7. Would you tell the truth even if it gets you fired?
   – Faith Popcorn – Faith Popcorn's BrainReserve

8. You can have the power but not the title
   – Mary Wells Lawrence – Wells, Rich, Greene

9. The fantastic one
   – Jessica Alba – The Honest Company

10. Do it differently
    – Georgina Gooley – Billie

A WOMAN'S PLACE

1. From convent girl to the sweet smell of success
   – Coco Chanel – Chanel

2. Beauty and the two undertakers
   – Anita Roddick - The Body Shop

A WOMAN'S WORK

A WOMAN'S INTUITION

"The intuitive mind is a sacred gift and the rational mind its faithful servant. We have created a society that honours the servant and has forgotten the gift."

ALBERT EINSTEIN

In the past, intuition was often seen as fuzzy, unreliable, crystal ball gazing and had no place in business.

However, it is a powerful attribute, a skill. It can be likened to a type of high-speed super logic where the unconscious mind works faster than the conscious one. To have and be willing to listen to your feelings can be useful and insightful, especially in marketing, which is as much of an art as it is a science.

1. THE PLASTIC PEOPLE WITH PLASTIC SMILES

– EV JENKINS – OXO ADVERTISING/ J WALTER THOMPSON

Oxo is the leading stock cube brand in the UK and has been so for nearly a hundred years. However, despite a history of great advertising, in the early 1980s it had lost its edge.

Unfortunately for the brand, this was at just the time it was facing an increasingly difficult marketplace.

There was a general decline in meat eating, a rapid increase in the consumption of ethnic foods – not something with which Oxo was generally associated – growth in the cooking sauce market and ongoing competition from other stock cube and gravy granule brands.

J. Walter Thompson, Oxo's advertising agency, and its senior planner, Ev Jenkins, suggested a radical piece of research. The research wouldn't focus on a new campaign idea, or even the brand itself, but would investigate family life in the UK. It would explore what family life was really like in the 1980s and what people's reactions were to how families were being presented in the media. While such ethnographic research is now commonplace, it was the first time that a major brand had commissioned a study that went beyond the scope of its business.

Ev Jenkins' rationale was that Oxo should be positioned as being central to good home cooking, and that good home cooking was central to good home life.

This atypical research was conducted by Stephen Wells, and he recalls:

"When I asked these mothers about family life, they let loose with a deluge of the trials and tribulations of everyday family life – doing the washing, trying to dry it when it had rained every day, doing the shopping and still trying to make ends meet, working out what to cook and then trying to get the kids to eat ...

"Then, just as I was wondering why anyone had a family if this is what it was really like, one of the mothers would remember something heart-warming: their child's first steps, a drawing brought home from school, and suddenly everyone would be smiling."

This uneven balance of grief, offset with small but very precious moments of relief, was the reality of family life. Stephen christened it 'war and peace' but noted, "that there seemed to be a lot more war than peace."

The second key finding was that, in the early 1980s, broadcast media was moving ahead of advertising. Programmes such as *Butterflies*, which humorously depicted a mother's attempts to cope with two teenage sons, and the soap *Brookside* were starting to reflect the reality of everyday life much more honestly than advertising.

Advertising at the time was full of perfect families, made up of attractive mums, handsome dads and children who were always immaculately behaved. A respondent in the research christened them "Plastic people with plastic smiles."

What the research clearly identified was that Ev's initial insight had real potential; there was an opportunity for a brand to reflect more accurately what family life was like.

Based on these two key insights, Ev briefed the JWT creative team, who developed what was to become one of the most famous and effective food advertising campaigns of all time. Launched in 1983, it ran until 1999.

2. DOING HER HOMEWORK

– MELITTA BENTZ – MELITTA COFFEE FILTERS

By the beginning of the 20th century, coffee drinking was no longer a luxury. Melitta Bentz and her husband, Hugo, were among the many people who had recently started to drink it daily, with their breakfast, with cakes and while just sitting and chatting in the afternoon.

However, Melitta's enjoyment was marred by the trials and tribulations of brewing a really good cup. The percolators were prone to over-brew the coffee, espresso-type machines at the time tended to leave grounds in the drink, and linen filter bags were tiresome to clean.

She was sure that there must be a better way. So, she started experimenting with different materials – ones that would not require washing. In the end, her homework paid off – or perhaps that should be her son's homework paid off!

She noticed a piece of blotting paper he was using, which, despite absorbing some of the ink, finally let liquid through. Could this be the answer?

Using a nail to poke holes in the bottom of a brass cup, she then lined it, not with a linen bag but with a sheet of blotting paper from her eldest son's school notebook. The results were outstanding. Not only did the coffee taste significantly more aromatic, there were no more grounds in the bottom of the cup, and preparation was fast and simple.

There was no bag to wash, as you simply threw the used 'blotting' paper away.

Melitta decided to set up a business and, on 20 June 1908, The Kaiserliche Patentamt (Imperial Patent Office) granted her a patent. On 15 December 1908, she registered her own company, 'M. Bentz,' for the sale of coffee filters with the trade office in Dresden. Her starting capital was 72 Reichsmark cents. The company headquarters was a room in her apartment.

After contracting a tinsmith to manufacture the devices, they sold 1,200 coffee filters at the 1909 Leipzig fair.

Her husband Hugo and their sons Horst and Willi were the first employees of the emerging company.

In the 1930s, Melitta revised the original filter, tapering it into the shape of a cone and adding ribs. This created a larger filtration area, allowing for improved extraction of the ground coffee.

In 1936, the widely recognized cone-shaped filter paper that fits inside the tapered filter top was introduced and the brand continues to grow today, producing a variety of different coffee brewing instruments and owning multiple coffee roasteries.

3. THE MID-AFTERNOON SLUMP

– CASSANDRA STAVROU – PROPERCORN

"My father was a hopeless cook but made the best popcorn. Together, we'd spend hours playing with flavours and ingredients, impatiently waiting for each kernel to pop, so we could try out our latest recipe," says Cassandra Stavrou, co-founder of the popcorn brand Propercorn.

In 2009, Stavrou, then working in advertising, noticed that her colleagues were always hit by a mid-afternoon slump. "Everyone wanted a snack but all that was on offer was a rice cake, which is bland and boring, or a chocolate bar that's unhealthy. I noticed an opportunity for a snack that was tasty and good for you."

She wondered if popcorn might be the answer, and it was then that she remembered the popcorn maker her father had given her, his last present to her. "I still had it in the box and felt that was a nice extra bit of conviction I needed."

Stavrou was experimenting in her kitchen but she couldn't get the results she wanted. She wanted to find a way to season the popcorn, where each popped corn was kept moving as the flavour was applied, ensuring an even coating on each piece.

She solved the need for movement by buying a cement mixer and lining it with steel, but applying the flavour was still proving to be a problem. That was until one night when watching an episode of *Top Gear* when inspiration struck. "They would paint the cars with a special spray kit that gives the finest mist." She wondered if this might be the solution she was looking for. It was: "I bought one on-line and used it to apply the oil to the popcorn."

Having solved the flavour distribution problem, she was faced with another one. Having achieved the product she wanted, she needed to find a UK manufacturer who could make it in this way. "It took nearly two years," she says. "UK manufacturing wasn't set up to season popcorn in the way I planned to: tumbling on a really large scale. I was also young, with no proven track record. I would turn up at industrial estates and the people there would basically tell me to go home."

It was around this stage of the business that Ryan Kohn, a friend of her ex-boyfriend, came on board as co-founder. Ryan was, at the time, running his own property development firm.

Stavrou was, in fact, following the advice of another famous start-up entrepreneur, Richard Reed of Innocent fame. He had told her, "You don't have to do it on your own. It's good to be accountable to someone."

Ryan's mother pumped £30,000 into the business, and they launched Propercorn with four flavours, including Sweet & Salty and Sour Cream & Chive in October 2011.

Their first customer was the café at Google's London office. Ryan explains, "I had a mutual friend who worked at Google and he put us in touch with the chef." Out of the 48 snacks on sale, Propercorn proved the most popular. "That was the first stat we had, and we went to Leon, Chop'd, Benugo and told them. It caught their attention," Ryan says.

The brand is now available in most major UK retailers and elsewhere all over the world, experimenting with first-to-market new products, and shows no sign of slowing down.

4. WALKING THE 'DOGS': HOW JO THOUGHT, NOT BOUGHT, HER WAY TO SUCCESS IN THE US

– JO MALONE – JO MALONE & JO LOVES

Jo Malone has launched not one but two famous fragrance brands.

"The similarity is that they both have the same mother," she says. "They both have that person that wants to push boundaries and say, 'I know it's always been like that, but what if …?' I live a life of 'what if?'"

She has faced numerous challenges along the way, one of which was the launch of her original 'Jo Malone' brand in the US.

At the time, she had limited resources and, looking back, she recalls, "When you are an entrepreneur and you have no money, you have to think, and you have to turn on a sixpence."

It was 1998, and following the success of her first store in Walton Street, London, an early fan, Dawn Mello, president of famous luxury Manhattan retailer, Bergdorf Goodman, offered a deal to open a concession in the Fifth Avenue store in 1998.

It was an opportunity that was too good to miss. So, Jo travelled to New York but arrived with only "1,000 bags and products" and no real marketing budget. She knew it was going to be a real challenge. "I sat there in a hotel room thinking: 'I am going to fail, what am I going to do?'"

It was time to start thinking.

Malone's inspiration came from something she had seen in her first few days in the States. She came up with an ingenious idea about how to create some noise without actually spending any money on advertising. "We [Jo and her husband Gary Wilcox] called it walking the dogs."

What the couple had noticed was how the socialites, rich and famous women, liked to walk along the sidewalks of fashionable streets with numerous well-branded shopping bags over their arms. Malone contacted 50 people she knew and asked them to take one of her bags for a 'walk' every time they left their homes and went out and around the fashionable districts.

A simple and effectively costless strategy paid off handsomely. "These bags started to be recognized in really savvy parts of New York City, so when we opened the store people thought there was already a store somewhere. There wasn't. There were empty bags wandering around New York City."

A year later, Estée Lauder bought the brand. Malone stayed on as creative director until 2006, when she stepped down after recovering from breast cancer.

She launched her second perfume business, Jo Loves, in 2011, but this time, she didn't need to rely on an empty bags stunt to gain publicity.

Footnote: When Jo Malone published her autobiography, Jo Malone: My story, *she insisted it had a fragrant twist. A page near the front is treated with Pomelo, a crisp, citrus-based scent from her Jo Loves collection.*

5. THE BILLION-DOLLAR BUTT

– SARA BLAKELY – SPANX

Sara Blakely believes she may be the only woman in the world who is actually grateful for cellulite and back fat. She says it was the reason behind her drive to turn $5,000 she had saved from selling fax machines into a $250-million-a-year business.

Whenever she is asked where that idea for her business came from, she says with delightful honesty: "My inspiration was my own butt."

Working in the hot Florida climate, Blakeley disliked the appearance of the seamed foot on her tights, especially when she wore open-toed shoes, but she liked the fact that their control-top eliminated panty lines and made her body and her butt appear firmer.

When cutting the bottom off normal pantyhose didn't work (the cut-off material on the legs rolled up too much), she started a search to find the right material. Eventually coming upon a solution in a craft store, she wrote her own patent following instructions from a Barnes & Noble textbook, and incorporated her company under the name Spanx.

Not only candid, she is clearly committed to her cause. Once she had her first samples made, she looked up companies in the Yellow Pages to find potential stockists. Having identified Neiman Marcus as exactly the sort of store she wanted to sell Spanx, she set off to convince the buyer of the merits of her new pants.

Blakely believes in the power of a product demonstration, and it wasn't long before she was in the restroom showing off her inspirational butt, demonstrating what it looked like before and after putting on Spanx.

It was a demonstration that got Spanx its first listing, albeit in only seven Neiman Marcus stores.

When an excited Blakely told the Spanx sample manufacturer about the Neiman Marcus deal, his response wasn't quite the one she had been expecting. He clearly wasn't as convinced of this being the beginning of something big. Blakely recalls him saying: "I thought these were just going to be Christmas gifts for the next five years."

Blakely, however, was determined that Spanx was going to be a success, and she wasn't going to leave anything to chance. She started to call up everyone she knew who lived near those first Neiman Marcus stores and asked them to buy a pair of Spanx, promising that she'd reimburse their money. Her reasoning was that if they sold well there, Neiman Marcus would extend their distribution.

It was still taking time to convince them. As Blakely recalled at Fortune's Most Powerful Women Summit in 2013, "Right when I was running out of friends and money … Oprah named them as one of her favourite things."

That changed everything. Distribution spread quickly to Bloomingdales, Saks and Bergdorf Goodman. In 2001, she signed a contract with QVC, the home shopping channel, where she sold 8,000 pairs in the first six minutes.

Blakely is now the world's youngest female self-made billionaire, according to *Forbes* magazine.

And I can almost hear Blakely saying she is the woman with the first billion-dollar butt.

6. THE PARTY WITH EXTRA TOYS

– JACQUELINE GOLD – ANN SUMMERS

In 1981, Ann Galea was working for Pippa Dee, a clothing company that sold its wares through parties organized in people's homes. She had just arranged for a party to take place in the front room of her house in Thamesmead, Essex, when she had an idea. She decided to ask her friend, Jacqueline Gold, to bring along some of the merchandise from where Jacqueline worked.

Now, Jacqueline Gold's merchandise was more than a little unusual. She was working for her father's sex shop business at the time, so Galea asked Gold to bring along some sex toys, hoping it would spice up the event.

Looking back on the evening, Gold remembers: "It was like a Tupperware party, but at the end of the evening, out came the toys. The girls' reactions were amazing. Suddenly, everyone was having fun and giggling. I could see there was a market."

Despite being just 21 and low on work experience, Gold developed a radical business plan for what was, at that time, effectively an adult publishing and mail order company that happened to own a couple of shops. Her radical plan was based on selling sex toys to women in an environment where they would feel relaxed – at a party in a friend's house. Chatting to the women after the Pippa Dee party had made Jacqueline realize that, while women were just as interested in sex as men, they didn't want to visit or be seen visiting the sex shops of the time.

On hearing the plan, one board member was supposedly outraged, declaring, "Women aren't interested in sex," but thanks to support from her father and uncle, Gold's plan was given the go-ahead.

The first party organizers were recruited through advertising and seminars held in the Strand Palace hotel in London. "I had to tweak the ad," recalls Gold. "I couldn't say ladies only and couldn't use erotic; it had to be 'exotic.'"

The first Ann Summer's Party generated £85 of sales. There are now some 7,500 party organizers who hold more than 4,000 parties every week. What's more, Gold no longer has to advertise for organizers. Applicants come to her.

She went on to further transform the organization into a successful online business, a chain of women-friendly sex shops on the UK high street with operations in the UK, Ireland, Dubai and Australia. The company, which had an all-male board and an £83,000 annual turnover, now has a board of which 70% are women and reached a turnover in the region of £140 million in 2018. Sounds like it's time for a party to celebrate her success.

7. JUST ANOTHER SECRETARY?

– BETTE NESMITH GRAHAM – LIQUID PAPER

Bette Nesmith Graham hadn't wanted to be a secretary. She was much more interested in art, in painting and drawing. However, after the war when she and her first husband divorced, she found herself as a single mum needing to find a way of supporting herself and her young son, Michael.

So, she became a typist and got herself a steady job at Texas Bank & Trust, earning $300 a month.

Like all secretaries, she made the occasional mistake when typing but hated rubbing out the type, as this often led to dirty marks on the page or, at worst, torn sheets. She was sure that there must be something better.

Inspiration came from her love of art. She remembered that painters covered up mistakes not by erasing their work, but by painting over them. This gave her the idea for a new way of tackling the problem.

Using her kitchen blender, she mixed up some tempera water-based paint, tinting it to match her company stationery. She took it to the office in an empty nail varnish bottle along with a small watercolour brush, and whenever she made a mistake on paper, she simply painted over it, 'fixing' the error.

It wasn't long before the other secretaries at the bank found out about her secret correction fluid and began to ask her if they could have some. Nesmith Graham began making up more bottles, putting labels on them that proudly displayed her chosen brand name, 'Mistake Out.'

Nesmith Graham soon realized that the product was popular enough to form the basis for a business. She started the Mistake Out Company in 1956.

At the time, she couldn't afford the $400 fee to copyright that original name but went on working on the product itself. "During that time, I often became discouraged," Nesmith Graham told *Texas Woman* magazine in 1979. "I wanted the product to be absolutely perfect before I distributed it, and it seemed to take so long for that to happen."

The business began to grow, and she started to employ her now-older son and his teen friends to fill bottles and put labels on them for customers. She paid them $1 an hour.

She now had two jobs: one as executive secretary for the chairman of the board and the other as chairman and CEO of Mistake Out, but she kept the second secret, as the bank wouldn't have approved. Indeed, when Nesmith Graham accidentally signed a bank letter with the name of her private company, they fired her.

It was perhaps a blessing in disguise, as it allowed Graham to focus her time and energy on her business. She finally applied for a patent for her product, which was now renamed Liquid Paper.

She was selling around 100 bottles of Liquid Paper per month when, in 1957, a magazine called *The Office* mentioned the product, and General Electric placed a large order. The business took off.

She married Robert Graham in 1962, and he joined the business as well.

By 1967, Liquid Paper was a million-dollar enterprise. In 1968, Nesmith Graham opened a new plant with 20 employees. That year, she sold one million bottles.

In 1975, Nesmith Graham divorced her husband, who had tried to wrestle control away from her. Later that year, she opened an even larger 35,000-square-foot headquarters building for Liquid Paper in Dallas.

Nesmith Graham was innovative in establishing her company culture, not only encouraging employees to participate in making corporate decisions, but based on her own experience she set up an in-plant library and child-care centre. She also used a portion of her earnings to set up two foundations to help women in need: the Gihon Foundation, established in 1976, and the Bette Clair McMurray (her maiden name) Foundation, founded in 1978.

In 1979, she sold her company to the Gillette Corporation for $47.5 million. A year later, she passed away at the age of 56.

Looking back on her extraordinary achievements, her son Michael, who had gone on to become the guitarist for the 1960s band The Monkees, said in a 1983 interview with David Letterman: "She had a vision, she had a lot of help, she married again and had some help [from] some capable execs, but she built it into a big multimillion-dollar international corporation and saved the lives of a lot of secretaries."

8. RESTORING THE PRIDE IN THE BRAND

– ANGELA AHRENDTS – BURBERRY

'Growth is good' sounds like a go-to marketing rule but the story of one famous British brand suggests otherwise, and it was a woman who identified and then rectified the problem.

That brand's story begins in 1856, when a 21-year-old former draper's apprentice called Thomas Burberry opened a store focusing on outdoor clothing. In 1880, he introduced gabardine, a hardwearing, water-resistant yet breathable fabric into his jackets and coats.

In 1911, Burberrys, as it was then known, was chosen as the outfitter for Roald Amundsen's expedition to the South Pole. Perhaps the biggest turning point for the brand came in 1914, when Burberrys was commissioned by the War Office to adapt its officer's coat to suit the awful conditions in Belgium and France. The result was the trench coat.

After the war, the trench coat became popular with civilians and, in the 1920s, what was to become the iconic beige Burberry check was created. It was used as a lining in the best-selling trench coats.

In 1955, Burberrys was taken over by Great Universal Stores, which instigated a period of innovation in a drive for growth. Base products like the trench coat, the Piccadilly raincoat and the cashmere scarf were all relaunched, all with much greater focus on the Burberry check. Burberrys became one of the most sought-after luxury clothing brands in the world, worn by a host of stars including Humphrey Bogart, Audrey Hepburn, Peter Sellers and Ronald Reagan

During the 1970s, 1980s and 1990s, in an effort to exploit the appeal of the brand, Burberry started signing more and more licensing agreements with manufacturers from all around the world, to (mass-) produce new and (what they hoped were) complementary items. These included suits, trousers, shirts, sportswear and accessories but also pet-ware, baseball caps and buggies. Nearly all featured the beige check.

However, as the new century arrived, the image of the brand started to decline, rapidly and dramatically. Burberry went from being perceived as a premium, luxury brand to one that anyone and everyone could, and did, wear.

Burberry became associated with 'chav' culture, a term defined in the Oxford English Dictionary as "a young lower-class person who displays brash and loutish behaviour and wears real or imitation designer clothes." The availability of lower-priced products and the proliferation of counterfeits that 'borrowed' Burberry's check, as well as the brand's adoption by B, C and D-list celebrities and football hooligans, wasn't consistent with an exclusive premium image.

A much-publicized photo of a former 'star' of the television soap opera *EastEnders* in 2003 prompted one commentator in *The Scotsman* to write, "Admirers of Burberry's trademark check sighed and slung it to the back of the wardrobe after Daniella Westbrook, a self-confessed addict, publicly overdosed on Burberry."

In 2006, there were changes at the top of Burberry. Rose Marie Bravo, the chief executive who had led the brand to mass-market 'success' through licensing, retired.

Angela Ahrendts replaced her, and when later interviewed by the *Harvard Business Review* for their January–February 2013 issue, she remembered the early days of her tenure.

"When I became the CEO of Burberry in July 2006, luxury was one of the fastest-growing sectors in the world.

"With its rich history, centred on trench coats that were recognized around the world, the Burberry brand should have had many advantages.

"But as I watched my top managers arrive for our first strategic planning meeting, something struck me right away. They had flown in from around the world [in]to classic British weather, grey and damp, but not one of these more than 60 people was wearing a Burberry trench coat.

"I doubted that many of them even owned one. If our top people weren't buying our products, despite the great discount they could get, how could we expect customers to pay full price for them?"

She was quick to identify the root of the problem.

"[Burberry] had lost its focus in the process of global expansion. We had 23 licensees around the world, each doing something different. We were selling products such as dog cover-ups and leashes. One of our highest-profile stores, on Bond Street in London, had a whole section of kilts. There's nothing wrong with any of those products individually, but together they added up to just a lot of stuff – something for everybody, but not much of it exclusive or compelling.

"In luxury, ubiquity will kill you – it means you're not really luxury anymore – and we were becoming ubiquitous."

There was no central control, different factories around the world were doing their own thing and, in many cases, they didn't even feature coats. Ahrendts set about changing things.

She appointed the designer Christopher Bailey as the 'brand czar' and gave him the ultimate say in the brand look and feel. Bailey recounts, "I told them, 'Anything that the consumer sees – anywhere in the world – will go through his office. No exceptions.'"

She closed the factories in New Jersey and Wales – the latter had been making polo shirts – and began reinvesting in the Castleford facility, which made the heritage rainwear. She and Bailey also took the brand back to its origins.

"When I became CEO, outerwear represented only about 20% of our global brand business. Fashion apparel and check accessories were leading our strategy.

"Surveying the industry, we realized that Burberry was the only iconic luxury company that wasn't capitalizing on its historical core. We weren't proud of it. We weren't innovating around it.

"The decision to focus on our heritage opened up a wealth of creativity. Christopher and the designers and marketers all started dreaming up ways to reinforce the idea that everything we did – from our runway shows to our stores – should start with the ethos of the trench."

They removed the brand's iconic check-pattern from all but 10% of the company's products, bought themselves out of the licensing deals and even out of the Spanish franchise that was worth 20% of group revenues.

A bold and brave strategy that hurt at first but then started to pay dividends – big dividends.

In that same 2013 *Harvard Business Review* interview, Ahrendts could proudly claim, "Today, 60% of our business is apparel, and outerwear makes up more than half of that. At the end of fiscal 2012, Burberry's revenues and operating income had doubled over the previous five years, to $3 billion and $600 million, respectively."

She also noted that pride in the brand had returned too.

"If you [now] ask a Burberry senior executive how many trench coats they own, the answer is likely to be eight or nine. Everyone has a packable version. Everyone has a white one. Everyone has an evening one. We have all different lengths. As for me, I don't have an exact count, but I can safely confess to owning a dozen."

9. A TAGLINE IS FOREVER

– FRANCES GERETY – DE BEERS/NW AYER

In the 1930s, presenting a woman with a diamond engagement ring when proposing was not the social norm it is today. The Great Depression had made matters even worse for De Beers, the brand that controlled 60% of rough diamond output.

De Beers decided to embark on what they now describe as a 'substantial' campaign, linking diamonds with engagement. They hired Philadelphia-based advertising agency N.W. Ayer in 1938 to try and make Americans fall in love with diamond engagement rings.

At the time, only 10% of engagement rings contained diamonds, and they were seen as an extravagance for the wealthy. Sales, already declining for more than two decades, had plummeted during the Great Depression.

The challenge Ayer faced wasn't easy and as internal Ayer documents later observed, the campaign required "the conception of a new form of advertising, which has been widely imitated ever since. There was no direct sale to be made. There was no brand name to be impressed on the public mind. There was simply an idea — the eternal emotional value surrounding the diamond."

The new campaign was to weave together two strands.

The first strand was to suggest a diamond's worth and manage expectations as to what to a man should pay for a diamond engagement ring. In the 1930s and 1940s, this was thought to be equivalent to a single month's salary (a figure that increased to two months in the 1970s and 1980s and more recently has become three months' salary).

The second strand happened in 1947 when, at a routine morning meeting, Frances Gerety, a young copywriter, suggested a new tagline. Her colleagues weren't particularly impressed. The all-male group felt it didn't mean anything and that it wasn't even grammatically correct.

Gerety, who had been working on the De Beers account since 1942, had often explored ideas of eternity and sentiment. Her previous ads, which had appeared in publications like *Vogue*, *Life*, *Collier's*, *Harper's Bazaar* and the *Saturday Evening Post*, had suggested things such as, "May your happiness last as long as your diamond" or "Wear your diamonds as the night wears its stars, ever and always … for their beauty is as timeless."

Her new line, "A Diamond is Forever," was the summation of her thinking and was the turning point in the campaign. "A Diamond Is Forever" first appeared in a 1948 ad and has appeared in every De Beers engagement advertisement since then.

By 1951, Ayer was seeing success and informed De Beers that "jewellers now tell us 'a girl is not engaged unless she has a diamond engagement ring.'"

In 1956, Ian Fleming's 1956 novel, *Diamonds Are Forever*, the fourth in the James Bond series, was published and subsequently turned into a film with a memorable theme tune of the same name sung by Shirley Bassey.

In 1999, *Advertising Age* proclaimed it the slogan of the century: "Before the DeBeers mining syndicate informed us 'A Diamond Is Forever,' associating itself with eternal romance, the diamond solitaire as the standard token of betrothal did not exist," the magazine explained. "Now, thanks to the simple audacity of the advertising proposition, the diamond engagement ring is de rigueur virtually worldwide, and the diamond by far the precious gemstone of choice."

By the end of the 20th century, 80% of engagement rings contained diamonds because, as all husbands know, she's worth it.

10. SOME LITTLE THING THAT MIGHT BE KIND OF USEFUL

– CAROL LATHAM – THERMAGON

You are a highly competent 50-year-old woman, a single mother of three with a bachelor's degree in physical chemistry. You have a hunch and then produce some hard data to support your theory. You think this could be a major business opportunity. You take it to your direct bosses and even try the executives at other business units in your company, but they all aren't interested. They claim they have other priorities and, frankly, some of your colleagues with their doctorates think you lack credibility, especially as the application is in an area you know little about – computing.

What do you do?

Well, if you're Carol Latham, you follow your instincts and set up your own company.

Latham was a staff chemist at British Petroleum (BP), and her gut feeling was that the future of keeping computer parts cool wasn't ceramics, as most of her colleagues believed. It was actually going to be plastics. If she was right, then Latham thought she could help solve one of the biggest problems that computer makers faced: how to dissipate heat that's produced by the components.

She set about backing her intuition with hard data; working out of BP's research lab in Warrensville Heights, Ohio, she explored how heat conductors, plastic- or polymer-based compounds compared with ceramics. Her results were everything she could have wanted. "I was getting eight to ten times higher thermal conductivity numbers than any polymers cited in the scientific literature," she would later recall.

Believing she was onto something, she took her idea and her data to her bosses with the request to launch a commercial venture under the aegis of BP. Nothing happened. "To get a large company to make a decision is very, very difficult," says Latham. "Basically, I was held in limbo."

Timing may have played a part in the decision or, rather, lack of decision. In 1987, BP had just become sole owner of Sohio. Oil stocks were sagging industrywide. Struggling to integrate Sohio and ride out the price slump, BP's management chose to concentrate on the company's core oil business and the capital and the appetite for other projects like Latham's was scarce.

Latham tried again and again, first to people higher in the R&D group, then other BP business units. "I wanted to turn this into a business," says Latham. "And BP perceived that it was just some little thing that might be kind of useful."

In 1989, she left BP and started her own company. She was convinced that her basic concept was solid and felt in her bones that she could develop that concept into an actual product.

As with many entrepreneurs, she had to do most things herself, from planning to marketing, to selling herself and her idea, as well as the ongoing product development.

She drafted and redrafted a business plan. Off the back of that she raised an initial $70,000 from family, angel investors and friends. Meantime, she was also working long hours in her home's basement using a kitchen blender, cookie sheets, and mixing bowls to try to turn polymer-based compounds into something commercial.

She found some very cheap workspace at a factory and moved herself and her family into a studio apartment so she could rent out her house.

She developed and implemented a very targeted marketing campaign. Aiming at West Coast computer manufacturers, she sent news releases and papers to technical journals.

If that wasn't enough, she did some part-time consulting work to help with her income.

By 1992, Latham had samples of an actual product – super-thin polymer sheets that she cut to fit between computer components.

After all the hard work, things took off quickly. The products, she says, "Basically, they sold themselves." She quickly built up an enviable client list including Intel, IBM and Silicon Graphics.

It had taken her three years to raise $100,000 in capital; now, investors were fighting to come on board.

Thermagon changed the microchip industry and, within five years of its launch, achieved sales of $18 million annually. At one point, Thermagon's thermally conductive materials were installed in more than 50% of the laptop computers made today.

Not bad for someone who followed her intuition and invented some little thing that proved to be kind of useful.

GIRL POWER

"Behind every woman is a tribe of other women who have her back."

ANONYMOUS

Women inspire other women. They help, they listen, they comfort, they push. In short, women help women. In fact, women help people. They help them do more, achieve more and be more. For many women, their greatest achievement isn't only financial or professional success but the people they have helped and inspired along the way.

1. THE QUEEN OF TUPPERWARE

– BROWNIE WISE – TUPPERWARE

In 1956, the *Houston Post* reported: "It has been estimated that Brownie Wise has helped more women to financial success than any other single living person."

But who was Brownie Wise and what was the brand on which her and so many other women's success was built?

Brownie's was born in rural Georgia. Her parents divorced and, as a teen, she travelled with her mother, who organized union rallies. It was on these trips that Brownie started giving speeches and soon proved to be an extraordinarily gifted and motivating orator.

The next stage on her path to success started with a bad door-to-door salesman. When a Stanley Home Products salesman knocked on her door and proceeded to deliver a terrible sales pitch for cleaning supplies, Wise scoffed and said she could do better.

By coincidence, Stanley had just started experimenting with home parties as a sales method and the salesman said if Brownie was so sure of herself why didn't she show them what she could do. She jumped at the chance and started selling Stanley products at parties. Before long she was making enough money to quit her secretarial job. She continued to rise up through the ranks, and she was soon in management and hoping to ascend even higher. However, those aspirations were quashed at a meeting with Stanley' head,

Frank Beveridge, who told her she'd never become an executive. Its halls were "no place for a woman," he said.

She was furious and started to look for other opportunities. It was a near-accident at a sales meeting that was to give her inspiration. One of her co-workers had seen some plastic storage tubs gathering dust in a department store and decided to bring them in. At first Wise didn't think they were anything special, but when she accidentally knocked a bowl off the table, it bounced instead of breaking, and the contents remained safe inside. Brownie saw the potential there and then.

She left Stanley and, in 1949, started throwing parties to sell Tupperware. It was a move that was to spark a mini-revolution; Tupperware didn't just help extend the life of leftovers, it was to become a career maker for Brownie and millions of other women.

Many of the women who came to one of Wise's parties were convinced not only to buy the products but to become Tupperware salespeople themselves.

As she hosted more and more parties, Brownie discovered more and more ways to convert women into Tupperware loyalists and advocates. She found that putting people on waiting lists, something she was initially reluctant to do, actually made them more eager to buy.

She quickly amassed outstanding sales but, more importantly, she started to build her team of more and more salespeople, and they in turn built their own networks. Soon, other Tupperware parties were taking place across the country. Wise's team in Detroit was selling more Tupperware than most department stores. This soon attracted the attention of the founder of the Tupperware Corporation, Earl Silas Tupper.

He offered her a promotion: distribution rights for the entire state of Florida. In the spring of 1950, she moved south with her son and mother.

However, things didn't go as smoothly as she hoped; there were disputes over turf with other distributors, but what annoyed her most was that she was constantly contending with botched orders, shipping delays and product shortages.

In March 1951, Wise had had enough. She called Tupper in a fury and demanded action – this was hurting not just her bottom line, but also his. Tupper listened and assured her that he'd fix the issues but wanted a favour: to hear her sales secrets and thoughts on growing the business.

The next month, the two met at a conference on Long Island and Wise explained her belief in the power of parties where people could touch Tupperware, squeeze it, drop it and seal it in the company of trusted friends or neighbours. With regard to growing the business, her suggestion was radical: ditch department stores altogether and focus entirely on throwing home parties.

Tupper took the advice to heart and the day after their meeting, he created a new division just for home parties and asked Wise to be the general manager. The halls of Tupperware executives weren't closed to women. Her stellar track record continued – she was selling more Tupperware than anyone anywhere.

The new approach saw Tupperware sales rocket, and wholesale orders exceeded $2 million in 1952. Tupper increased her salary to $20,000 and, on her birthday in 1953, he presented her with a gold-dyed palomino horse. He also gave her the freedom to do practically whatever she wanted.

Wise started travelling the country recruiting, presiding over sales conferences and announcing contests and doling out prizes as an incentive – including, sometimes, her own clothes.

The beauty of selling Tupperware at parties for many women was it allowed them to be employed, yet not appear to challenge their husbands' authority or the status quo in what was still a very traditional, male-dominated world. The parties allowed women to contribute to their family's bottom line. Wise embraced the spirit of female entrepreneurship wholeheartedly, she wrote a newsletter called Tupperware Sparks, published a primer called Tupperware Know-How, and had a 52-minute film, *A Tupperware Home Party*, made as a training tool

Wise had become the face of Tupperware, the result of her success but, unfortunately, it also sowed the seeds of discontent with Tupper. In 1954, she was the first woman to appear on the cover of *Business Week*. The magazine's profile was glowing, to say the least. It credited Wise and her sales technique with Tupperware's estimated $25 million in retail sales while seeming to downplay Tupper's role as president of the company he had created.

Tupper had never craved the spotlight for himself; in fact, he was known to use the back door of his office. He believed the focus should be on the product and not the employees. After the *Business Week* article, Tupper sent a note to Wise: "However good an executive you are, I still like best the pictures … with TUPPERWARE!"

It was the beginning of the end. Their relationship started to deteriorate and, in 1958, Tupper fired Wise. After a heated legal battle, she received only $30,000 as a settlement. She had no stock in the company.

Tupper ordered her name expunged from the company history. Later that year, he sold the company to Rexall Drug for $16 million.

Wise tried starting new companies but never achieved the same success she had with Tupperware. She ended up leading a quiet and content life, knowing she had contributed so much to the financial success of so many women. She died at her home in 1992.

2. DON'T LET THEM GRIND YOU DOWN

– WENDY GORDON – RESEARCH BUSINESS

Wendy majored in psychology and social anthropology in her native South Africa and got a job working for a management consultancy. They wanted to set up a market research arm, and she recalls that somehow, she was selected to join the new team and got to work.

"I knew fuck all about [market research]. Somehow, I got through some sort of selection criteria – to my amazement. The first year, I was setting up a whole market research unit, recruiting black interviewers who were schoolteachers across the country, teaching them how to do a questionnaire, how to ask questions. It was fascinating. I did that for three years."

Unfortunately, an embarrassing turn led her to leave. "My boss at the time got drunk one Christmas party and told the whole company that he was in love with me." He was sacked but, feeling somewhat awkward, she decided to move on. So, she joined an established research agency where she learned the basics of quant research.

Her next move was prompted by a wish for new challenges and a desire to do both qualitative and quantitative research. She decided to move overseas and came to the UK. She took her time and spoke to a number of the leading agencies of the time finally choosing to join Schlackman.

Looking back, she says, "I chose [to join] Bill. I don't know why. There was something about the way he interacted with me. I liked Bill and his quirky ways, and that's how I really got into qualitative research."

It was here that she met and started working with Colleen Ryan, and together they would transform the standard approach to qualitative research. They had a feeling that qualitative research needed to evolve. At that time, most qualitative research projects took six to eight weeks to complete. Speaking to advertising planners, such as Judy Lannon at J. Walter Thompson, they soon realized they had been right and there was a demand for much faster turn-around times. They decided that by working together things could be done much quicker and, ultimately, they could help advertising agencies and their clients make their decisions on campaigns much faster.

"We'd do projects together – we'd do the first groups together, then I'd go north and do two groups, she'd do two groups somewhere else – then we'd get together and figure out what was going on. We would work out which route they should go with, which advertising execution – what was it communicating, what did they like."

The prevailing attitudes of the time weren't done with Wendy yet. Having left Shlackman's again, she was contacted by a couple of advertising agencies, as there were strong links between research and planners and experience as a researcher was a frequent path into planning. One agency she spoke to was Allen Brady and Marsh. She had three interviews and all seemed to be going really well, but then she had to meet Peter Marsh.

As their interview was drawing to a close, Peter asked, "Come on, Wendy, what would you do in this scenario – we have a pitch over the weekend and your daughter is in hospital, where would you be?" Wendy immediately replied, "In hospital, of course." As Wendy says, looking back, "That was it. This [attitude and expectation] was just endemic at that time."

In the end, Wendy and Colleen decided the best thing was to do it for themselves, and they created The Research Business.

It was a huge success, doing really, really well – making money, delivering what their clients wanted and building their team. "We couldn't believe how much money we were making," Wendy says, smiling

The smile fades as she then recalls, "At the MRS conference that year, John Goodyear (the MD of another major research agency) said, "Are you and Coleen having a lovely time making up your transcripts in the park?" The top ten market research companies were run by men. We were purely qualitative, and we had 120 people working for us. They said these things, like The Research Business wasn't credible and genuine. They somehow thought we had got there by cheating, making up interviews; that was hard trying to hold your own. And we weren't alone – [other women faced] those snide, snarky, aggressive comments, getting a pat on the head."

However, for Wendy and Colleen, it didn't knock them off their stride; it just made them want to carry on.

And that's what they did. The business was hugely successfully. When Wendy realized that she was spending too much time running the business, not doing it, and Colleen decided she wanted to sail around the world, they sold the business and moved on.

Asked to look back on the experience, Wendy not surprisingly and quite rightly sees it as an achievement.

"What I'm proud about is that we created an amazing company that was really successful, a good place to work, enabling of women, women who wanted to have children, women who were pregnant – I'm immensely proud."

3. NOT PLAYING THE FIELD, LEVELLING IT

– WHITNEY WOLFE HERD – BUMBLE (& TINDER)

After her first experience, Whitney Wolfe Herd had no real plans to return to the world of online dating, but back she went, and what she created has helped transform the market.

At age 22, Wolfe Herd had joined Hatch Labs, and through them she became involved with a start-up called Cardify, which was a project led by Sean Rad. The project was abandoned, but through the connections she had made, Wolfe Herd joined a dating app start-up with Rad and Chris Gulczynski.

Wolfe Herd became Vice President of Marketing for Tinder. The name was her idea, a combination of the flame logo and her practice of having used tinder to start fires at her father's cabin in Montana. She is also credited with building its popularity by focusing on college campuses to grow its early user base.

Two years after joining, however, Wolfe Herd left the company, suing for sexual harassment. Despite a reported settlement of more than $1 million, she became the subject of abuse.

It became so bad that, looking back, Whitney Wolfe Herd remembers being in a "perpetual state of sheer and utter anxiety. I did not want to leave my house." She was a target for misogyny at levels she didn't realize existed. "Hate was just coming at me at all times," she said. "I always knew toxic masculinity was an issue, but I'd never seen it at such scale."

So, not surprisingly, her next idea was nothing to do with dating. Instead, she worked on an idea of an online social space for women. She pitched her idea to Russian billionaire and the founder of dating app Badoo, Andrey Andreev. He wasn't taken with the idea but liked her "passion and energy." He suggested she return to her area of expertise – dating apps.

Wolfe Herd pitched numerous other ideas before presenting one Andreev was willing to back.

Looking back in an interview with Clare O'Connor for *Forbes* in November 2017, Wolfe Herd remembers her pitch: "What if women make the first move, send the first message? And if they don't, the match disappears after 24 hours, like in Cinderella, the pumpkin and the carriage? It'd be symbolic of a Sadie Hawkins dance – going after it, girls ask first. What if we could hardwire that into a product?"

Andreev loved the idea of putting women in control and agreed to put up an initial $10 million for approximately 80% of the company. He also agreed to let Wolfe Herd have access to Badoo's software and systems.

Bumble was born in December 2014 and clearly struck a chord with many women; the app had 100,000 downloads in its first month.

Bumble's feminist approach to dating and Wolfe Herd's flair for marketing shone through its advertising. Billboards read, "Be the CEO your parents always wanted you to marry," and "We're not playing the field, we're levelling it."

Bumble quickly became America's fastest-growing dating app with users growing 70% year-over-year. It now has over 25 million users.

In 2016, Bumble launched BFF, an app that is meant to help women find friends, not dates.

It followed this up with Bizz, which focused on women meeting other women for the purpose of career networking.

Bumble is run by a majority-female executive team and is now reportedly valued at more than $1 billion, and Wolfe Herd was named one of *Business Insider*'s '30 Most Important Women Under 30 In Tech in 2014.' In 2016, she was named as one of *Elle*'s 'Women in Tech.' She was named in *Forbes*' '30 under 30' in 2017 and 2018.

4. TO BOLDLY GO WHERE NO BARBIE HAS GONE BEFORE

– SAMANTHA CRITOFORETTI – ESA AND MATTEL/BARBIE

Samantha Cristoforetti is currently the only active female astronaut in Europe, which is a pretty good claim to fame and makes her a role model for lots of children, but especially young girls.

Unfortunately, unless they are already into space travel, they might not know this.

Fortunately, Cristoforetti now has another claim to fame. Thanks to a partnership between the European Space Agency (ESA) and toy manufacturer Mattel, she has been made even more famous, as she has been immortalized in a one-off (or, to be precise, 'two-off') Barbie dolls.

As part of their Dream Gap project and in partnership with the ESA, Mattel created two special Barbie dolls. Each is a likeness of Cristoforetti; one has her wearing a stylized reproduction of NASA's Extravehicular Mobility Unit, or Spacewalking suit, and the second has her in an ESA blue flight suit.

They were first shown by Mattel Italia at a special event on International Day of the Girl on 11 October 2018, and in 2019 they have been on display at the Women's Day Gala of Professional Women International in Brussels, the ELLE magazine Power Girl event in Paris and many other events.

They have generated huge amounts of PR on social media, TV and in the press, and will be supplemented with a series of videos aimed at young girls and their parents. They show Cristoforetti welcoming girls from the UK, Germany, France and Italy into the ESA European Astronaut centre in Germany. The girls shadow her and ask her all about her extraordinary day job.

As Isabel Ferrer, European Director of Marketing for Barbie and clearly one never to miss the opportunity for a pun, said: "We are proud to launch this collaboration with the ESA with a clear goal: to inspire girls to become the next generation of astronauts, engineers and space scientists. We know how important it is for girls to have role models and this new ESA collaboration helps us take this to an astronomical new level."

Only 15% of active astronauts are female, and no woman has ever landed on the moon, so the partnership fits perfectly with the Barbie Dream Gap Project, which aims to level the playing field for girls and close gaps so they reach their full potential.

It is a similar hope for the ESA, Ersilia Vaudo-Scarpetta, Chief Diversity Officer, said: "While boys and girls generally achieve the same scores in science and maths, few girls dream of becoming scientists, engineers or space professionals. The European Space Agency is strongly engaged in promoting girls' interest in STEM subjects and space careers in particular, as we need a diversity of talents to imagine and enable the future in space. We are therefore proud to launch ESA's collaboration with Barbie, highlighting inspiring role models such as astronauts and encouraging girls to believe in themselves, look at the sky and dream high."

Cristoforetti, who understands the importance of role models, said she hoped the partnership with Barbie "will help young girls and boys to dream about their future without limits."

5. HEADS OR TAILS

– JEAN AND JANE FORD – BENEFIT

After graduating from Indiana University, Jean and Jane, six-foot-tall identical twins, moved to New York to try to break into the modelling world. While they got some I. Magnin and Macy's catalogue work, they had to supplement this with sales clerking and apartment cleaning.

So, in 1973, they decided to move to San Francisco. "I came to find a husband," Jane later admitted, while Jean felt she needed to move before she was shoved. As Jean says, "I came because I'd burned every bridge with my partying. Oh, honey – reckless abandon. I loved every minute of it. Whatever happened to Quaaludes? Those were great days."

A year later, they got what was to be their most famous modelling assignment as the girls in the Calgon Bath Bead commercials. "They'd wanted blonde twins," the distinctly brunette Jean says, "and couldn't find any that could talk. So, they showed us a script and said, 'They can speak! Sign them up!' It was a major gas."

A couple years later, and after receiving a stern 'Don't waste your education' letter from their mother, they decided they'd better try to put their modelling to good use. After much discussion, it came down to two ideas. Unable to make up their minds, they agreed to leave the final choice to chance – the toss of a coin: heads, they'd open a casserole café; tails, a cosmetics store.

Tails it was, and in 1976 the sisters opened the Face Place in San Francisco's Mission District.

The transition from beauty store to cosmetics brand started soon after with an unusual request from an unusual customer.

In an article in *Elle* in 2011 by Holly Hillea, Jean picked up the story …

"One morning, a worn-out stripper walked into the store. Her shirt, some tie-dyed thing. The fishnets broken up. She was wasted. She put both arms on the counter, and she said, 'Hiii.' Drunk. She said, 'I need somethin' special,' something to keep her nipples pink. Apparently, whatever she was applying was wearing off mid-performance because, 'when I dance, I sweat.'

"So, Jane and I looked at each other and said, "We have that. It's just not here right now. Come back tomorrow. Jane came over to my apartment, and we got a bunch of red food colouring, glycerin, rose petals … and we put it in the blender and boiled it down to a reduction. It was so strong!"

They poured some into two little glass vials that had corks in them. Jane drew a rose and added the words 'rose tint,' and they glued it onto the bottles.

Jane recalls, "The gal comes in the next day – same outfit – to get her goods. She came back a week later and said, 'I've run out, and all my friends want it.' She said, 'My tribe needs this.' We said, 'Friday, we'll have 24 more bottles for your weekend.'"

From there demand took off and, as Jean remembers, it was initially a very targeted crowd. "Strippers, ballerinas, gay guys, all coming in: 'I want that rose tint,'" but soon it began selling to a much wider audience. It was renamed Benetint in 1990 and is now marketed as a lip and cheek stain. It is still the brand's bestseller with over ten million bottles sold to a clientele that now includes Sarah Jessica Parker, Nicole Kidman, Kate Hudson and romance novelist Danielle Steel.

The brand is now known globally as Benefit, and it's not just a brand by women for women but one that lives by the girls' own quirky philosophy, perhaps best summed up by the line from their Benefesto – "We believe laughter is the best cosmetic."

6. **FINDING YOUR PASSION**

– DEBBIE STERLING – GOLDIEBLOX

Debbie Sterling was a woman in search of her true passion. She recalls, "I graduated from Stanford in 2005 with a degree in engineering and product design. On my graduation day, I was incredibly fortunate to be in the audience during Steve Jobs' famous commencement speech, which brought tears to my eyes. He told us all to never settle until we found our passion. From that day forward, I set out to find my passion. The problem was, I had no idea where to start!"

Debbie's early career was to encompass a stint at a branding and design agency, a life-changing experience working for the VSO in rural India and working as the marketing director of a small jewellery company called Lori Bonn. While she enjoyed her time in each of the roles and learned a huge amount along the way, she knew deep down she still hadn't found what she was looking for.

In the end, she found her passion during a brunch. Talking to *Business Insider* in 2016 she recalled:

"I had started a club with my friends called 'Idea Brunch,' where once a month we'd get together, cook a big breakfast and each person would get up in front of the group and share their latest idea.

"My friend Christy, who had studied engineering with me in college, got up and started complaining about the lack of women in our classes. She mentioned how she used to play with her brother's construction toys when she was young and how that inspired her early interest in engineering. Her idea at Idea Brunch was engineering toys for girls.

"It was then that I finally had my 'Eureka!' moment because I knew instantly that it was my true passion ... what I had been searching for ever since Steve Jobs' speech."

Sterling knew that promoting STEM (science, technology, engineering, and mathematics) careers to girls wasn't going to be just painting Lego bricks pink and that she would need to overcome resistance and even prejudice.

She started researching the subject and the first myth she addressed was the general assumption that boys outperform girls in maths and science. Sterling found out that, actually, the opposite was true everywhere but North America and Western Europe.

"[Many people] suggested the reason girls and women don't enter engineering is a biological reason ... that boys are inherently better at maths and science, and that's why there are no girls in engineering and there was nothing I could do to change that," said Sterling.

Next, she turned her attention to the toy industry and children's media, meeting with neuroscientists and preschool teachers, and observing kids play.

"I came up with an 'aha' that construction toys do really help develop spatial skills and are a good precursor for engineering, but they have been heavily marketed toward boys for over 100 years" and that she would need to tailor any construction toys for girls.

Her next 'aha' moment was the realization that girls have naturally inherent verbal skills. "Girls really love stories and narratives ... It became really obvious to me that the way to get girls engaged in engineering and building was to incorporate a narrative."

Sterling now needed to translate her insights into an idea. Her creative leap was to apply those insights and recognize that the heart of her offer shouldn't be about toys, but rather it should be based around a 'character franchise,' similar to children's icons like Dora the Explorer. The offer would, of course, include toys, but would also feature cartoons, video games, merchandise and apparel. The franchise had a very particular mission to "disrupt the pink aisle."

Sterling launched GoldieBlox in 2012 and the first character, Goldie, was introduced in a combined storybook and construction set teaching girls how to build a belt drive. The inspiration for Goldie came from the "kind of funky, brave, but not perfect girl characters" that Sterling had grown up with. Characters like Pippi Longstocking and Matilda.

However, almost immediately she started to meet resistance. "When I first began prototyping Goldie, the first girl engineer character, and building the business, the toy industry wasn't receptive. I spoke to several people that told me it was a 'noble cause,' but it would never go mainstream and it wouldn't sell. They all said boys like building, girls like dolls – and that you can't fight nature. It was disheartening to hear, but I knew they were wrong."

So, she turned to crowdfunding platform Kickstarter to help get the backing she needed and put up a video telling the story of GoldieBlox. It went viral and within three months GoldieBlox raised $1 million in pre-orders on Kickstarter.

"I've heard time and time again that that video brought people to tears, for many reasons, and many people connected to it in different ways," Sterling said. "It wasn't just parents, it was [also] some more progressive toy store buyers, anyone with a daughter or anyone who has ever felt underestimated or made to feel stupid in not being capable to do maths or science. Nobody likes being put in a box, nobody likes being stereotyped, and I think that video really got at that."

By 2017, GoldieBlox has had more than one million app downloads and sold more than one million toys across more than 6,000 major retailers worldwide. It has been named one of *Fast Company's* Most Innovative Companies and The Toy Industry Association's 'Toy of the Year.'

Talking to *Forbes* in October 2017, Debbie said, "It's now been six years since I quit my job to start GoldieBlox, and I still wake up every day incredibly passionate about getting girls interested in engineering and technology."

7. WOULD YOU TELL THE TRUTH EVEN IF IT GETS YOU FIRED?

– FAITH POPCORN – FAITH POPCORN'S BRAINRESERVE

"I had a very, very strong maternal background. My grandmother collected rents in seven languages. My mother was a negligence lawyer in the 1920s. The women in my family are [metaphorical] 'cowgirls.' They didn't even know the word 'feminist,' they just were," so says perhaps the world's most famous futurologist, Faith Popcorn.

She launched her company, Faith Popcorn's BrainReserve, from a New York studio apartment when she was just 27 years old. She remains its CEO over 40 years later, and the company now has a reputation for helping companies protect and prepare their products and services and work out their investments and business plans for the future, and how they can deal with unexpected reversals in the market.

She herself describes her role as "saving clients from the future if the future is against them."

Popcorn is fiercely proud of their process. "It's not fluffy," she says. "We have a 32-step methodology." They have talent bank of 10,000 futurists, "braille the culture" continuously, conduct interviews, reading and watching everything they can.

They also have a way with words and have coined the phrases 'cocooning' (staying home), 'cashing out' (quitting the rat race) and 'down-aging' (acting youthful) – just a few of the many trends they helped identify and popularize.

Popcorn and her team claim with a 95% accuracy rate and not surprisingly have a blue-chip client list that includes American Express, Bayer, Campbell's Soup, GE, Johnson & Johnson, Kellogg's, KFC, SC Johnson, Tylenol and The United States Postal Service.

Popcorn is also the best-selling author of books including *The Popcorn Report*; *Clicking*; *Eveolution: Understanding women – eight essential truths that work in your business and your life*; and *Dictionary of the Future*. She has been called "the trend oracle" by *The New York Times* and "the Nostradamus of marketing" by *Fortune* magazine.

However, in interviews she often talks about her honesty and directness (her cowgirl traits). While she thinks of them as two of her strengths, not all her clients agree with her about that.

Sometimes clients don't want to hear or believe what she says.

"In 1981, we said people will be buying from the internet and that supermarkets would be much less interesting. We talked to P&G and others, and to say they laughed at us is an understatement. How did we figure that out? A multitude of interviews with mainly female customers who were going to supermarkets and telling us how much they hated them. We had interviews and conferences with people that were inventing the pre-Amazon pre-delivery services. We could visualize easily a day where everything will be delivered and ordered on the internet."

And her honesty has even got her fired on more than one occasion.

"We were hired by Kodak. Our assignment was exactly this: what is the future of film? We went through our process, interviews, talent town bank, put a big team on it. And we came back and we said the future of film is digital. They said we didn't hire you to tell us that, we hired you to describe the feature film. I said, but digital is the future. And they said you're fired. That's happened a couple times, [where] I'm fired for, I guess, telling the truth. So that was very depressing. But I move forward by saying, am I going to make stuff up [to clients]? No."

She recognizes that the truth can be painful but still firmly believes honesty is the best policy. "Every client I've ever had that's been a successful relationship said it might have been painful, it wasn't easy, but we're very happy that we engaged, and we were prepared. We told John Tyson that vegetarianism was coming. I'm not saying that he was thrilled to hear this, but that was the truth."

And what trends has she been talking about recently? Well, they have included 'emonomics,' which provides some suggestions for brand managers in a post-truth world, where people are media and marketing savvy. Popcorn suggests that marketing can tap into the fact that people are "predictably irrational." If a brand, or even a presidential candidate, can capture what we're thinking and saying, giving voice to our raw emotions, it can pull us in despite ourselves and what we know to be true.

As one commentator recently said, "Popcorn has big, interesting and quite possibly accurate predictions to offer. Her connection to corporate culture, her intuitive grasp of marketing, and her unique position as a woman in a role dominated by men give her a leg-up on her competition." Now, that's the truth if ever I heard it.

8. YOU CAN HAVE THE POWER BUT NOT THE TITLE

— MARY WELLS LAWRENCE — WELLS, RICH, GREENE

When told by her boss that he could give her the authority to do whatever she wanted but couldn't offer her the title of president because, if he did, "No one would come." Mary Wells Lawrence left and set up her own advertising agency.

It would prove to be phenomenally successful, and Lawrence would go on to become the first female CEO of a company listed on the New York Stock Exchange.

Mary Wells Lawrence was born Mary Georgene Berg in Youngstown, Ohio. Her career began as a copywriter at McKelvey's, a local department store, but she relocated to New York City, and in 1953 became a copywriter at the advertising agency McCann Erickson.

Four years later, she joined Doyle Dane Bernbach, where she helped create some famous campaigns including, "Plop, plop, fizz, fizz" for Alka Seltzer. It was Lawrence's suggestion that the ad show two, not just one tablet being put into the glass. This subtle nudge that people should use two tablets helped further increase sales. Other memorial ads she wrote for Alka Seltzer included, "I can't believe I ate the whole thing" and "Try it, you'll like it."

After DDB, Lawrence went to work for Jack Tinker and his agency, Jack Tinker and Partners. It was a revolutionary agency, more like a think tank, and was affectionally called 'Tinker's Thinkers.' It was here she helped develop "The End of the Plain Plane" for Braniff International Airways, working with copywriter Dick Rich and art director Stewart Greene. Her idea was to reflect the cultural mood of excitement and vitality and the sense of a world opening up, a vibrant contrast to the dull aesthetic of most airports and airlines at the time. She recommended dressing the stewardesses in Pucci and painting the planes in pastel colours. It was a campaign that helped turn around the business.

That and other successes helped build her reputation, and in 1966 she felt that she could rightfully ask to be made president. Her boss, Marion Harper, declined. He offered the power but not the presidency.

Looking back, she recalls, "He could see that I was feeling a red rage, and he said, 'You wouldn't want to ruin something you built,' and at that point I just walked out the door."

She left, along with two trusted colleagues, and founded Wells, Rich, Greene. They set up temporary offices in a hotel; Braniff left Tinker for the new enterprise, and Lawrence's mother took charge of the phones.

By the end of its first year, Wells, Rich, Greene had 100 employees and $39 million in billings.

In 1967, Mary Wells, as she was then, married Harding Lawrence, the president of Braniff International Airways, the agency's largest client. Wells, Rich, Greene resigned the Braniff account on principle, avoiding any charges of conflict of interests.

In 1968, the now Mary Wells Lawrence took the agency public, and in the same year she became the youngest person ever to be inducted into the Copywriters' Hall of Fame. By 1976, she was earning more than $300,000 a year, making her one of the highest-paid US female executives.

In 1990, she sold the business for $160 million.

As a successful woman, she was asked what drove her success. Her reply then is still good advice today: "You can't just be you. You have to double yourself. You have to read books on subjects you know nothing about. You have to travel to places you never thought of travelling. You have to meet every kind of person and endlessly stretch what you know."

In 1999, Lawrence was added to the Advertising Hall of Fame by the American Advertising Federation, which called her "the force behind one of the most creative shops in the history of advertising."

9. THE FANTASTIC ONE

– JESSICA ALBA – THE HONEST COMPANY

Jessica Alba would appear to have a head start when it comes to building a brand. She is an A-list actor, starring in films like *Sin City* and *Fantastic Four*, and has some 50 million followers on social media.

But, despite her fame, Alba discovered that creating her vision for a brand that would mean that you didn't have to choose between what works and what's good for you wasn't easy and at times, "I just felt so alone on this journey," she told a CNN podcast *'Boss files with Poppy Harlow.'*

The idea for The Honest Company started shortly after Alba had an allergic reaction to a baby detergent she was using to clean onesies for her first child. "I just felt like how the heck could something that's marketed to babies specifically and all of that give me this type of reaction. Like, what's going on?"

Alba started searching for safe, eco-friendly and affordable childcare products. She found it incredibly difficult to find any products that met her high standards.

So, in 2009, she developed a business plan and pitched it to numerous funds and individuals. She got no takers.

Still believing that she was on to something, she spent the next few years researching the eco-friendly consumer goods market. Following her appearance in Washington, DC, where she was lobbying for updated legislation to reform the 1976 Toxic Substances Control Act, she connected with Brian Lee, Sean Kane and Christopher Gavigan. They were to become her co-founders.

The business had a clear mission, expressed as The Honest Standard: "Performance and peace of mind: meaningful transparency and thoughtful design. We're on a mission to change the world, one product at a time."

While sales were good, there were tensions, and Alba felt that at times the business wasn't consumer-centric enough.

"The issue was, you know the mindset was, that when you build something from nothing, you're really having the business revolve around a business model, versus building a brand and being consumer-centric. So, there was this tension, which I think probably could be a healthy tension initially when you start something, but ultimately if you want to build something that's going to last, you have to build a brand and you have to think of the consumer first, and that's what I got back around to."

What made the situation even more difficult for Alba was that she was 'outnumbered' by the men. "It's tough when you're the only woman in the room, in the board room," she says. "It's not that they didn't want to [add women to the board], but when you're thinking month to month about your financial goals, that's more important than building a long-term vision and strategy. It's just a different mentality on how to build something."

Alba's husband, Cash Warren, reminded her of the importance of listening and learning but, ultimately, she knew "there's also a point where you've got to put your foot down."

"You have to trust your gut, and you have to know that diversity and thought is important … I shouldn't be the only one who understands the consumer and cares about the consumer."

This and other business setbacks led to changes at the company.

The business was hit with several lawsuits, had to instigate some voluntary product recalls and, in early 2017, 80 people lost their jobs. Steps were taken to address the issues.

There was a change in leadership, and Nick Vlahos, a former Clorox COO, became the new CEO. Alba says he shared her view on consumer-centricity. "That's how he thinks about building a brand."

They decided to scale back production on some of their newer products and refocus on the core products that drove the company's initial growth: childcare, beauty, lifestyle and diapers, in particular.

They also decided to bring R&D (research and development) and QA (quality assurance) in-house. They wanted complete oversight of the manufacture of their products. "We do our own formulas in-house, and then we work with manufacturing partners to make it at scale," Alba explains. "That's very differentiating compared to others in the marketplace, where they normally [rely] on a third-party manufacturer to help cocreate the formulas."

Business performance responded, and the brand is back in growth.

Looking back, Alba recognizes that failures can be important learning experiences. "I think the most valuable lessons actually come from making mistakes and going down the wrong path."

The changes weren't finished there. While 65% of The Honest Company's 400 employees are women, only three of nine executives (including Alba) are female. Alba led the charge to help women rise up within the company.

"We're also creating a program inside of the company, so no matter where you come in, at any entry-level job or up, there's a path for you ... to get you up to where you want to go in your life, and up to that C-suite executive capabilities.

So we're going to have a curriculum, and a program and a mentorship in-house, inside of The Honest Company, for women specifically. It's necessary."

That programme, The Honest Company's first employee resource group, WELL (Women Excelling in Leadership and Living), has now been launched.

10. DO IT DIFFERENTLY

– GEORGINA GOOLEY – BILLIE

Georgina Gooley doesn't do the obvious. When she and her co-founder, Jason Bravman, launched their new female shaving brand, their first campaign promoted not smooth, silky legs but female body hair.

The Project Body Hair Campaign was a deliberate choice. In an established market with entrenched existing players, Gooley knew she had to do things differently, but perhaps, just as importantly, she wanted to make a point she truly believed in. For her, this wasn't about being different for difference's sake.

"We created Project Body Hair because we wanted to acknowledge that women have body hair and celebrate the fact that it's our choice whether or not we choose to remove it."

For her, the fact that the competition has consistently shown women shaving what were already smooth, hairless legs was senseless. "By refusing to acknowledge that body hair exists, the industry was body-shaming women, making them feel that the best version of themselves is when they have hairless bodies," Gooley says.

The campaign has been a huge success with over 22 million video views and press coverage across 23 countries.

The competition's ads weren't the only thing that outraged Gooley; their pricing did, too. For years she had used men's razors because she refused to pay the 'pink tax.'

"The pink tax is a sexist pricing strategy where products that are marketed toward women are more expensive."

Her aim was to create products that "are priced fairly." In the shaving market, women were paying 10–15% more for razors than men. Gooley thought this was both "offensive and totally absurd." She decided things had to change.

"We knew that women were frustrated with the prices of razors, and we were determined to give them a premium shaving experience that was half the price of the competition and priced directly in line with affordable men's razor subscriptions."

They also committed to donating 1% of all revenue to women's causes around the world.

This drive to be different was there from the start. Looking back, Gooley reflects that "building a company from scratch starts by asking yourself two simple questions: why would anyone care you exist? And, how are you going to differentiate yourself? Through our research, not only did we want to differentiate ourselves in terms of quality and price, but we also set out to build a very different kind of relationship with women, compared to what other razor companies had done in the past."

This understanding of the need to differentiate her brand stems from her early career. She had spent time working at advertising agencies in Sydney, New York and Portland, Oregon, and was fascinated by brands and understanding why some brands resonate more than others.

She and Bravman talked about some basic differences like those between men and women. They decided that there might be an opportunity to create a brand that prioritizes women in a category that was traditionally male dominated. They identified the shaving market as an obvious candidate and initial research helped convince them they were on to something. They found that most shaving companies had been created for men or have been spun out of men's brands – women appeared to be an afterthought.

Once they had set their direction, Gooley and Bravman knew they had to stay true to it so while working on the products, their website and the campaign, they made sure that they kept focused on their vision. "There are always a million little and big things that can distract and even deter you from getting to launch. It's important to have a north star and remain goal-oriented, focused, persistent and imaginative."

They launched in November 2017, a year after they had the original idea, with starter kits that included a Billie razor, a magnetic holder and two five-blade razor cartridges. They also launched with a range of body care products. Recognizing that their Body Hair Campaign could essentially make its products obsolete, they wisely decided they needed a broader offer.

They were an immediate success and hit their 12-month targets in their first few months.

While Gooley says she loves the positive customer feedback, for her what has been even more exciting is seeing how their stance has encouraged other women's razor brands to also show body hair and to talk about shaving as a choice versus something that women are expected to do. It's proof that a new, challenger brand like Billie could change the way women are represented in a very traditional category.

Perhaps not surprisingly, she has become even more of a champion of brands that put women first. She is passionate about creating products and experiences that make everyday life "a little more delightful" and maybe "a lot more affordable" for women. In recent PR interviews, she shares her views on the key success factors for creating women-first brands. They are:

1. Do your homework
2. Have a different point of view
3. Change the conversation
4. Celebrate real women
5. Think like a consumer (not a marketer)

Good free advice!

A WOMAN'S
PLACE

*"A woman's place is in the kitchen ...
sitting in a comfortable chair, with her feet up,
drinking a glass of wine and watching her
husband cook the dinner."*

ELIZABETH GILBERT

A woman's place is where she wants it to be.

And in many cases, her place is to challenge, to change things, to make things better, to do things in a different way. Women are catalysts for change. To quote Dolly Parton: "If you don't like the road you're walking, start paving another one."

1. FROM CONVENT GIRL TO THE SWEET SMELL OF SUCCESS

– COCO CHANEL – CHANEL

Gabrielle Bonheur 'Coco' Chanel was the daughter of a market-stall holder and a laundry woman in Saumur, Maine-et-Loire, France, but after her mother died, she was sent to a Cistercian convent where she would spend her teenage years.

In 1909, she arrived in Paris as the mistress of the textile baron Etienne Balsan. She set up a millinery boutique under Balsan's apartment and, by 1920, she had become a phenomenon in French fashion circles. She ran a series of successful boutiques in Paris, Deauville and Biarritz and was the belle of Parisian elite society. But she still wanted more. She was fastidiously clean, and later, when working with many of her clients, she would complain about the way they smelled, stinking of musk and body odour.

She decided to create a scent that could describe the new, modern woman she epitomized – "a woman's perfume, with a woman's scent" – and once Coco Chanel had decided something, she went about achieving it.

During the late summer of 1920, Chanel went on holiday to the Cote d'Azur with her then lover, the Grand Duke Dmitri Pavlovich. There, she learned of a perfumer, a sophisticated and well-read character called Ernest Beaux who had worked for the Russian royal family and lived close by in Grasse, the centre of the perfume industry.

Beaux took up Chanel's challenge, and after several months he had come up with ten samples that he presented to her. They were somewhat randomly numbered to anonymize them – one to five and 20 to 24.

One of the samples, whether by mistake or design, a question which is still the matter of some debate, contained a larger than normal dose of aldehyde. This was unusual because in those days the normal way to create fresh fragrances was to use citrus such as lemon, bergamot and orange but none of these lasted on the skin. Chemists had isolated chemicals called aldehydes that could artificially create these smells but, as they were very powerful, perfumers were hesitant to use them.

Chanel chose the sample with the aldehyde. "It was what I was waiting for. A perfume like nothing else," she would later say.

It was a formulation that probably subconsciously appealed to her desire for cleanness and freshness.

And the number of the sample: No. 5, of course.

To celebrate, she invited Beaux and other friends to a popular upmarket restaurant on the Riviera and sprayed the perfume around the table. It is said that every woman who passed the table stopped and asked what the fragrance was and where it came from. She was now certain she had another success on her hands, or rather her neck.

And while the brand is now famous for its celebrity endorsement from the likes of Marilyn Monroe, Catherine

Deneuve, Suzy Parker, Candice Bergen, Lauren Hutton, Nicole Kidman, Audrey Tatou and Gisele Bundchen, one of the first models used in the advertising was Coco herself.

2. BEAUTY AND THE TWO UNDERTAKERS

– ANITA RODDICK – THE BODY SHOP

In 1976, Gordon Roddick left for an expedition that was to take him from Buenos Aires to New York on horseback. He left behind his young wife, Anita. Anita needed some means of supporting herself and their young family while he was away and, after considering various options, she decided that she wanted to open a shop selling cosmetics.

This was to be no ordinary cosmetics shop; she was inspired by her earlier world travels and, in particular, by the practices of Tahitian women, who made cosmetics using local, natural products. She wanted to eschew the traditional glossy, highly-packaged, highly-advertised approach of many beauty firms.

She wanted to champion recycling, natural products, and a fair return for the producers of the all-important ingredients.

The store still needed a name. While travelling in America, Anita had seen a car bodywork garage named 'The Body Shop.' She had immediately liked the name and remembered it. A student created a logo for her for the princely sum of £25.

Her choice of name, however, wasn't popular with two undertakers who had premises close to her first store in Brighton. They thought the name might be bad for their trade, and she received a letter from their solicitors. Rather than give up on her new brand name, Anita decided to fight for it. She contacted the local paper and told them her story. They reprinted it in a double page spread, providing wonderful free publicity just in time for the store's launch.

On Saturday 27 March 1976, The Body Shop opened its doors to the public for the first time. The day's takings were £130.

Fast-forward 27 years, and The Body Shop now has more than 1,500 stores worldwide. The brand still doesn't use traditional advertising, although it exploits all the opportunities it gets to promote itself using its store windows, in-store posters and leaflets, lorries and any PR opportunities that arise.

Anita Roddick has appeared in a commercial, however. It was part of a campaign for American Express, where celebrities talked about how American Express helped them to conduct their business. Anita stuck to her principles of not spending her money advertising The Body Shop, but found another means of gaining free publicity for her brand.

3. WOMEN CAN'T EAT PRETTY PINK HEADLINES

– NATHALIE MOLINA NIÑO – BRAVA INVESTMENTS

Nathalie Molina Niño's life would make a great movie.

She is an amazing, multitalented woman, a successful serial entrepreneur, an advocate for women and an author.

At the age of nine and living in the US, she spoke better English than her Colombian mother or Ecuadorian father and so had to help them with managing their affairs and paying the bills. At college, as winter was setting in, Nathalie wanted a car but had limited funds. Having found one she wanted, she offered to pay for it half in cash, and half in trade by creating a website for the car dealership. She already had a student job at the university's computer labs, which had enabled her to learn how to code. The car dealer accepted and was so happy with her work that he told friends, who told others. Soon, she was building sites for larger companies such as Colorado Lottery.

She launched her first tech start-up at 20, and, by her mid-30s, she had already built four companies. It was then that she changed direction and took a degree in theatre from Columbia.

Niño had realized, "There were plenty of other engineers and technologists who knew what I knew or could learn what I learned and do it even better than I could. What was the secret sauce that made me uniquely successful, and would position me to succeed in the future? I found that it was storytelling. There were engineers who could code circles around me, but I was always the person who could explain complex concepts to anyone. I was good at creating narratives, and I loved doing it."

The course gave her the opportunity to go and learn and hone her craft with people she readily admits were "much, much better at it." It is now one of the reasons she believes makes her such a strong investor: "I invest in companies who want me to help craft their stories."

In 2012, Niño used her storytelling skills to help women-led businesses, co-founding Entrepreneurs at Athena at the Athena Center for Leadership studies of Barnard College. Its mission is to help level the playing field for female entrepreneurs, and she focused on investing in female entrepreneurs and women-led start-ups.

In 2015, she stepped in as chief revenue officer at PowerToFly, a company that connects women with jobs in tech. PowerToFly, in turn, helped lead to the launch of media mogul Nely Galán's SELF MADE movement, whose message to women is to become financially self-reliant through entrepreneurship.

From there, it was small step to launching BRAVA Investments, a company that aims to help grow start-ups and support businesses that disproportionately benefit women.

She realized that BRAVA needed to be different and their investment thesis isn't about investing in female-led companies.

"At BRAVA, we're looking at a wider problem set. I call our investment philosophy, 'outcomes over optics.' Which means we don't limit our investments to female-owned businesses;

instead, we focus on companies that benefit women, which is different. An investment in a female-owned company may make a nice headline (optics), but if all that investment does is make one woman very wealthy or worse, if that company harms the environment or perpetuates workforce abuses (outcomes), is it really moving the dial for women? This is why we prioritize outcomes, not optics. The other thing we focus on is true representation and intersectionality.

"We look for high-growth companies that do things like pay their mostly-female workforce living wages and give them benefits in industries that rarely do – think: elderly care, childcare, domestic workers, food."

BRAVA believes it should focus on investing in and buying from companies that truly, in meaningful and measurable ways, benefit all women they come into contact with. The wealth of one female billionaire, or even a dozen of them, isn't going to magically trickle down and benefit the billions of women who need it.

And master of the soundbite as well as the story, Niño says, "Women can't eat pretty pink headlines. Women, just like savvy investors, demand real, measurable outcomes."

Interviewed recently, Niño recounts, "My favourite example of a company we're researching is one that feels, at first glance, like it wouldn't fit at all. It's a company called Curemark, which has developed the first ever drug for kids with autism, and the FDA is fast-tracking approval for it to go to market. On the surface, it might seem like autism mostly affects young boys. Yet, if you view it as an economic issue, this drug can financially empower women. Let's start with the research that shows that most marriages involving kids with autism end in divorce. If you look at divorce, women usually take on the majority of the financial burden for raising children. This illustrates that sometimes all a company has to do to elevate women is to simply exist in the world. They don't need a public relations campaign about female empowerment or have a board full of women. It just so happens that this company has a woman CEO named Joan Fallon, but that's not why we are talking to them."

She has strong views on leadership: "A woman is most powerful when she allows herself to be supported. That is not something I have been good at for most of my life. If you asked me five years before I stepped down from my last company about what I thought power was, I probably would have said it's about outcomes, getting shit done, leading people like a 'herding the cats' kind of leadership. I don't think that is the case anymore. Allowing yourself to be supported means you work in a team environment rather than using a top-down approach. Sure, you might be the one with the CEO title, but acting as part of a team rather than separate from it means you're not as lonely and alone, and helps you to accomplish even more."

And if that's not enough for any movie producers out there – you can add in surviving cervical cancer, a successful book, *Leapfrog: The new revolution for women entrepreneurs* and possessing a secret power of not getting bitten by mosquitos, ever.

4. THE SUPERMODEL WITH SOCKS APPEAL

– KATHY IRELAND – KATHY IRELAND WORLDWIDE

Kathy Ireland was one of the elite group of 1980s supermodels; a group that included Christie Brinkley and Cindy Crawford. She may not have been quite as famous internationally as Chrissie and Cindy, but her career post-modelling suggests she was by far the most business-savvy.

She was scouted by Elite Model Management when she was 16 and became best known for appearing in 13 consecutive *Sports Illustrated* swimsuit issues. During *Sports Illustrated*'s 'Swimsuits 50th Anniversary' event, Ireland's 1989 cover was awarded "The greatest *Sports Illustrated* swimsuit cover of all time" by its publisher.

In 1993, now 30 and pregnant with her first child, she was approached by John Moretz, a marketer who asked if she wanted to model some socks. For some models this might have seemed like a step down or a sign that their best years were behind them. Kathy saw things differently. A natural entrepreneur, she made a counterproposal – a partnership to produce and sell her own brand of socks.

"I wanted to make it clear to them that I didn't want to just put my name on it," says Ireland. "An endorsement wasn't interesting to me."

Looking back, she recognized that, "It would have been easier to do a swimsuit line, but if I could put my name on socks and be successful, then I must really have something."

Equally open to new ideas, Moretz too could see the potential: "She's the girl next door who happens to be beautiful, that forms an emotional bond with the consumer." So, he bought the rights to use her name on a line of socks and agreed to pay for manufacturing and distributing the socks that Ireland would design and promote.

In return, Ireland would get a royalty on every pair sold.

She took out a $50,000 personal loan to launch kathy ireland Worldwide.

Moretz got her athletic socks into a number of sporting goods stores like Big 5. They did well enough for him to buy the rights to license exercise clothes, bodysuits and eventually swimwear.

Moretz became the master licensor for Kathy Ireland, sublicensing her name to companies that made things besides socks and collecting 30% of that revenue stream to Ireland's 70%.

His biggest coup of those early days was in helping her get an exclusive deal in 1994 with Kmart.

In 1998, thanks in part to some advice from her famous mentor, Warren Buffett (who appreciated their shared childhood experience as newspaper deliverers), Ireland decided to expand into furniture.

He told her that fashion changes, but the home remains far more secure, and that in apparel every celebrity already had a line or was pitching one. There was a market gap in home furnishings and so it proved as the kathy ireland range was a huge success.

Now, kathy ireland Worldwide (or kiWW, for short) has now grown to become one of the world's most valuable global licensors covering home, fashion apparel, wedding, fine jewellery, baby, children's toys and books, publishing, pet care, crafts and gifts. It is consistently ranked among the top 50 licensors. In 2015, it was number 31 on License Global's 'Top 150 Global Licensors' 2015 list with $2 billion in retail sales.

The brand's appeal may have been launched on Ireland's fame, but it is now built on providing products that are at once aspirational and relatable. kathy ireland Worldwide has thrived by imbuing the most unglamorous products with glitz, including desks, end tables, beds, headboards, rugs, carpets, ottomans, bookcases and windows.

She also has a real affinity for her core target audience. Perhaps her most famous quote is about the trials and tribulations facing busy moms: "Recognizing that, for a busy mom, getting in the car when you've got car seats and temper tantrums, [and] making it out the driveway is a victory. Making it into the store, that's heroic." The company's motto is, "Finding solutions for families, especially busy moms."

Interestingly, her commitment to her core audience is also reflected in the fact that she avoids store openings and many public appearances, despite her drawing power. "We've tried it, and it doesn't work," she says. "What happens is the store gets cluttered with guys who are there with 500-year-old copies of *Sports Illustrated*. How does that help a busy mom? These people are just in her way."

5. TO DYE FOR

– SHIRLEY POLYKOFF – CLAIROL/FOOTE CONE & BELDING

One of copywriter Shirley Polykoff's early accounts was Clairol, a brand that specializes in hair colour and hair care and which at the time of her appointment faced a number of challenges. Perhaps its biggest issue was that in the 1950s, having your hair dyed blonde marked you out as a good time girl. It suggested that you slept around.

This made Shirley Polykoff angry. She felt a woman should be entitled to do whatever she wanted with her body (and her hair!). Out of that anger arose the now-famous Clairol ad campaign. Shirley's aim was to turn around the image of blondes. She proposed using a Doris Day type, 'girl-next-door' blonde in the advertising, alongside the headline, "Does she, or doesn't she?" The subhead would read: "Colour so natural only her hairdresser knows for sure."

As Dave Trott, no mean (m)adman himself, said: "The brilliance was using that headline against those models – with a picture of a fresh, wholesome blonde, the answer wasn't so obvious." The girls looked too innocent to be sleeping around.

It was a very difficult campaign to sell and even harder for the client to buy. Many at the agency, Foote Cone & Belding, tried to kill it, and the clients weren't sure it was the right image for Clairol.

So, while everyone finally agreed to run the campaign, they were equally ready to pull it at the first sign of trouble. All of that changed when letters started coming into Clairol.

One particular letter stood out. It said: "Thank you for changing my life. My boyfriend Harold and I were keeping company for five years, but he never wanted to set a date. This made me very nervous. I am 28 and my mother kept saying soon it would be too late for me. Then, I saw a Clairol ad in the subway. I decided to take a chance and dyed my hair blonde, and that is how I am in Bermuda now on my honeymoon with Harold."

Everyone loved that letter. It was circulated around the entire company and used as the theme for a national sales meeting. The doubts about the campaign disappeared.

Over the next decade, the percentage of women colouring their hair rose from 7% to 40% and the image of blondes moved from being brassy to being fresh, confident and fun. The market grew from $25 million a year to $200 million, and Clairol took half of it.

But what made Shirley Polykoff a real genius in Dave Trott's eyes wasn't having the idea for the campaign but something that came to light many years later. At the leaving party for her retirement in 1973, a number of speeches talked about how her campaign had helped pave the way for women's equality and feminism. Shirley Polykoff stood up, thanked everyone and asked if they remembered the particular letter that had given everyone the courage to get behind the campaign. Of course, everyone smiled and nodded.

Shirley Polykoff said, "Actually, I wrote that letter."

6. MAYBE IT WILL GROW ON ME

– CAROLYN DAVIDSON – NIKE

One day in 1971, Carolyn Davidson, a design student at Portland State University (PSU), was sitting in a hallway working on a drawing assignment and bemoaning the fact that she couldn't afford to take an oil painting class. A young associate professor overheard her and asked if she wanted to do some work for him and his fledgling company. He offered to pay her $2 an hour. She accepted.

Phil Knight was that young associate professor of accounting at PSU. He had taken the job to supplement the modest income he made running Blue Ribbon Sports, Inc. – a small, fledgling company that served as a West Coast distributor of Japanese-made Tiger brand sneakers in the US.

Carolyn's initial work involved making charts and graphs for his BRS meetings with executives visiting from Japan. Phil, however, had bigger plans and wanted to start selling his own brand of cleated shoes for football or soccer, which he was having made in Mexico. He gave Carolyn a new brief. He wanted an identity, a stripe, which was the industry term for a shoe logo.

Phil told her it needed to convey motion and that it couldn't look like the logos of Adidas, Puma or Onitsuka's Tiger.

For the next fortnight, Carolyn worked on numerous ideas, the best of which she would sketch out by hand on tissue paper and lay them over a drawing of a shoe she'd done. In the end, she presented five or six of her designs to Phil and two other Nike executives

Unfortunately, they weren't that impressed and when her initial presentation closed, they asked, "What else you got?"

Carolyn said that was all she had to show.

Phil and his team were pressed for time and after discussion it became clear that all three men were at least willing to accept one of the designs. The checkmark they chose just happened to be Carolyn's favourite too.

Phil summed up his thoughts at the time, saying, "Well, I don't love it, but maybe it will grow on me." Because they needed it so quickly, Carolyn didn't even have any time to refine or clean up her initial design.

In 1972, the company first began selling shoes with the Nike name, named after the Greek goddess of victory. In June 1972, the first running shoes bearing the swoosh were introduced at the US Track and Field Olympic Trials in Eugene, Oregon.

For her services, she billed the company for 17.5 hours of her time ... $35.

She continued to work for Nike designing ads, brochures, posters and catalogues. As the company grew exponentially, there came a point in late 1975 when it became clear that her one-person design shop was too small to handle all of Nike's advertising and design needs.

Nike and Carolyn agreed it was time for a full-service ad agency. She opted to split her time homemaking and doing some freelance design work.

In 1983, three years after it went public, the executives at Nike surprised her with a party. In additional to presenting her with a gold ring in the shape of her swoosh, complete with a small diamond, they also gave her a certificate of appreciation and 500 shares of stock.

Of that gift, Davidson says, "It was something rather special for Phil to do, because I originally billed him and he paid that invoice."

She has never sold the shares and they are worth between $0.5–1 million today.

7. LET'S TALK ABOUT SEX

– CINDY GALLOP – MAKELOVENOTPORN

"I'm the only TED speaker to utter the words 'cum on my face' on the TED stage six times" is some claim to fame, but it is far from the only reason that Cindy Gallop, the ex-advertising guru and now adult industry revolutionary, is (in-)famous. She says of herself, "I like to blow shit up. I am the Michael Bay of business."

Most recently, she is the founder and CEO of MakeLoveNotPorn, a user-generated, crowdsourced website that is aiming to sexually "reeducate, rehabilitate and reorient" a younger generation raised on porn. On the site, in the profile section, she says she is captivated by taxidermy, Tokyo and William Gibson, loves sex and martinis, and is deeply grateful for younger men.

One of the reasons for that gratitude is that younger men were the inspiration for Gallop's latest venture.

Cindy (Lucinda) Gallop was born and educated in the UK. Her first job was as a theatre publicist, but after giving a talk, one of the attendees came up to her and said, "You could sell a fridge to an Eskimo." It made her wonder if another career might suit her better.

She joined the London office of British advertising agency Bartle Bogle Hegarty in 1989 and was soon responsible for large accounts like Coca-Cola, Ray-Ban and Polaroid.

In 1996, she helped start the Asia Pacific branch of BBH and went on to found the US office in 1998, where she was chair of the board. In 2003, Gallop won the Advertising Woman of the Year award from Advertising Women of New York.

She founded her own brand and business innovation consultancy, Cindy Gallop LLC, in 2006.

In 2009, she gave the notorious TED talk and launched the MakeLoveNotPorn.com.

Talking about the inspiration for both these ventures explains, at least in part, her gratitude for younger men. She had noticed in her own sexual encounters with younger men that they increasingly believed that real-world sex should mirror hardcore porn. In an interview with the *Independent* newspaper, she explained how this had sparked her entrepreneurial idea: "I thought, 'Gosh, if I'm experiencing this, other people must be as well ...' I'm a naturally very action-orientated person, so I went 'I want to do something about this.'"

She was worried about porn becoming the default form of sex education. Her subsequent four-minute presentation quickly became one of TED 2009's "most talked about" videos, partly due to her claim to fame quote. Its success helped kick-start the launch of the website.

It started as what she calls a "tiny clunky website" but now boasts 400,000 members globally.

Initially the website just listed "the myths of hardcore porn and balances[d] them with the reality." It evolved in 2012 to a video-sharing site – MakeLoveNotPornTV – based on the concept of 'real-world' sex. Nowadays, users can submit videos of their sexual encounters and rent videos of others. The videos are rented for a price, half of which goes back to those featured in the videos. There are now more than 800 videos and over 100 of what Gallop likes to call the MakeLoveNotPorn stars. The site uses a rent and stream model, rather than a download model because if any of those featured in a video decide they no longer want their private home video on the internet, the video can be immediately taken down. Any videos that do not convey "real world sex" or videos filled with porn clichés are rejected by the website's curator.

Gallop says her project is so different to porn because it is so much more than "masturbation material," and the mission of the website is bigger: "To help make it easier to talk about sex." "The core value proposition of MakeLoveNotPornTV resides in the fact that everybody wants to know what everybody else is really doing in bed and nobody does," Gallop told *HuffPost* in 2013.

She and the team would like to expand the brand into sex education forums and offer specially produced erotica such as film and art, though Gallop is finding getting the necessary funding difficult, as investors are concerned as soon as they hear the words 'adult content.'

Gallop argues, "We're not porn, we're not amateur, we're building a whole new category on the internet that's never previously existed: social sex. When I say social sex, think about all those celebrations of relationships that crop up on your Facebook timeline every day from friends: engagement announcements, wedding, lovey-dovey couple things. All we're doing is providing a platform to celebrate that last area of human relationships that nobody else will let you, but the motivations and social dynamics are exactly the same."

She's fighting the current norm that all variants of porn are categorized under "one big homogeneous mass," as well as the resulting stigma that leads people to hide their porn consumption.

So, she's using the approach she learned in her advertising career: using highly emotive, profane language, openly seeking attention and not being scared of polarizing opinion.

"You can quote facts and figures until you are blue in the face; but if any of those facts and figures worked, our industry would look completely different. Rational facts and figures do fuck all for this issue; you have to make it emotional. Our creative strategy at BBH was, 'We don't sell. We make people want to buy.'"

For example, she drew this provocative parallel in an interview she did with *The Independent* in July 2016: "Porn lacks socially acceptable curation and navigation; there is no Yelp of porn," she says. "[There is] no Yelp because it is ok to come by the office water cooler on a Monday morning and go 'I'm really bored of restaurants I'm eating at, who knows a new restaurant?' It is not ok to come in and go 'I'm really bored of the porn I'm watching, who knows some new porn?' and that's a problem. The landscape of porn needs navigation especially for younger people."

8. A 'GAMBOL' SHE WAS HAPPY TO TAKE

– LINDA MCCARTNEY – LINDA MCCARTNEY FOODS

Linda McCartney was an amazing, multitalented woman. She was a professional photographer. She was a talented musician and entertainer. She won an Oscar as cowriter of the award-winning song, 'Live and Let Die.' She became a well-known animal welfare activist.

She overcame the initial resentment of millions of young female Beatles' fans who were heartbroken when she married Paul McCartney in March 1969.

And if that wasn't enough, she became a successful author and entrepreneur.

The origins of the brand that was to carry her name began around the kitchen table. Sir Paul recounted the story to Nigel Slater in *The Observer*, 29 April 2007:

"We were in the kitchen at the farm, sitting down to the usual roast Sunday lunch, and through the window we could see all these little lambs, a great big gang of them, doing that cute thing that lambs do, you know, where they all run to one end of the field like this ... " At which point Slater says Paul stopped talking and did a quick lollop-y impersonation of the lambs gambolling, before continuing, "And then they all ran back to the other end of the field. They were having a great time. And we just looked down at the leg of lamb on our plates. We made the connection and that was it. Linda picked up the ball. We decided then and there to give up eating meat."

The second chapter of the brand's origins came about as Linda worked on ways to fill what the family call "the hole in the plate" – the place where the meat had formally been. She worked on a plethora of recipes, introducing her family and Paul to new ideas. "I'd never had quiche, it wasn't the sort of thing we grew up eating in Liverpool," Paul told Slater.

She soon had a collection of tried, tested and tasty recipes and approached a publisher who readily agreed to publish *Linda McCartney's Home Cooking*. It was subsequently published in the UK by the then fledgling publisher Bloomsbury in 1989 and sold 400,000 copies. It is still one of the best-selling vegetarian cookbooks ever in the UK. Subsequent books followed.

With increasing time pressure and improvements in the quality of prepared foods, Linda McCartney Foods was established by Paul and Linda. On 30 April 1991, at The Savoy Hotel, Linda McCartney and her family launched her meat-free brand.

The original range comprised a range of frozen vegetarian products including golden nuggets, ploughman's pie (cheese pie), ploughman's pasties, lasagne, Italian style toppers and beefless burgers. The recipes were based on dehydrated textured vegetable protein (TVP).

Some of the sales proceeds were to go toward McCartney to develop the range further and to fund her animal aid charity, Animal Line.

The packaging graphics were designed by Springett Associates and featured Linda McCartney's portrait and signature, a black-and-white illustration by artist Jonathan Mercer and the Vegetarian Society's seal of approval.

The ready meals were manufactured by frozen food company Ross Young's and were the first to not feature either the Ross or the Young's brand name.

Ownership of the brand has changed hands a number of times across the years. It became part of United Biscuits' McVitie's Prepared Foods division in March 1996. It was then sold in December 1999 to H.J. Heinz Co.

It was sold again in 2006 to the Hain Celestial Group. The McCartney family, however, remains involved in its development.

Sadly, Linda is no longer directly involved. In 1995, she was diagnosed with breast cancer and died from the disease in 1998 at the age of 56.

Her memory and her brand live on – on the current website it says: "An original food pioneer, Linda McCartney believed in great-tasting, honest, meat-free food and the shared pleasure that eating well could bring."

It goes on to say that those involved in the brand today, including the McCartney Family, are dedicated to sharing Linda's passion for wholesome cooking with everyone. "We are inspired daily by Linda's enthusiasm for celebrating life through good food. And so, our unique range never compromises on taste or quality and is made with care and compassion."

9. KICK SUGAR, KEEP CANDY

– TARA BOSCH – SMART SWEETS

Ben and Jerry started making ice cream after buying a $5 correspondence course. Things have clearly moved on since they sold their first ice creams in 1978.

Tara Bosch had to pay CA$90 (£54) for her heavy-duty gummy bear mould but used the internet to research alternatives to sugar.

Bosch grew up in Vancouver, British Columbia, and was, as she now says, a "sugar addict." She loved five-cent penny candy like Starbursts and Skittles that she bought from the local convenience store almost every day. One of her favourites were sour gummy worms.

Looking back, she says, "I had an unhealthy relationship with food, which affected my self-esteem and body image."

Bosch's emerging concerns about sugar were compounded in conversations with her grandmother. She learned how her grandmother regretted consuming so much sugar over the years and how it had impacted negatively on her quality of life.

"It was this conversation, coupled with my personal journey, that sparked my exploration into the shocking reality of sugar and how it's affecting society in a dramatic way."

Those findings confirmed that it was a major problem but also maybe a major opportunity. "On average, on any given day we consume in excess of 70 grams of sugar and Americans spend an estimated $1 trillion yearly fighting the damaging health effects of sugar, ranging from obesity to cancer. This is a large, urgent ... and valuable problem."

Bosch gave up sugar and set her own and her soon-to-be brand's purpose: to kick sugar but keep candy. She started experimenting in her kitchen using her gummy bear mould. It wasn't easy. Bosch recounts, "I think the trickiest thing about [gummy] candy is that 99% of it is sugar. So when you want to remove it, you basically have to start from scratch and recreate the product."

She spent up to 16 hours a day on her computer researching ingredients and ideas. She eventually found stevia leaf extract, which comes from the South American stevia plant. It is a very high-intensity sweetener because it's up to 200 to 350 times as sweet as sugar but doesn't have any calories.

Now the hours were spent trying recipes and, after 200 iterations, she found one she really liked. It combined the stevia with tapioca, which acted as a thickening agent, and chicory root to help create the gummy-like feel.

With help from her incubator programme, she raised the capital needed for her first production run and she then turned her energy to landing her first retailer.

She cold called and emailed so frequently that the store manager at Choices Market finally agreed to a meeting.

Despite all the time she had spent on getting the meeting, she nearly didn't attend. "When I arrived out front, I was so nervous that I drove away. Then I drove back, had the meeting, and they became the first retailer to take a chance on Smart Sweets."

That was in 2015, and since then other Canadian chains have started selling the brand, and in 2018 Bosch secured her first American customers. The US now accounts for 80% of Smart Sweets' sales.

Smart Sweets expects its 2019 revenues to exceed CA$50m (£30m). It is brand leader in the no- and low-sugar sweets sector in both Canada and the US and employs more than 45 people. Bosch, however, measures her success differently. "This year, we are helping people kick more than one billion grams of sugar," she says.

Bosch's self-assessment is relatively modest but, ultimately, for her it comes down to the power of three.

"For me, growing up, I wasn't that smart or athletic. I didn't really have any talents in particular, but I always had an innate sense of urgency, resourcefulness and the ability to make something happen if I decided I wanted to make it happen. Smart Sweets was the first time I realized the power of those three things combined."

10. THE BREAST PUMP AND THE CATWALK

− TANIA BOLER − ELVIE

You're launching a new breast pump and the question is: where do you hold the launch events?

In hospitals on maternity wards? At doctor's symposiums? In new parents' support groups? With leading retail pharmacy chains? At the London Fashion Week?

And the answer is, of course, London Fashion Week.

Well, it is if you're the radical new femtech company called Elvie, and what's more, you'll follow it up by installing four huge inflatable breasts around Shoreditch and the City "to encourage people to talk more about breastfeeding."

Tania Boler gained health degrees from both Oxford and Stanford and went onto do a PhD in reproductive health. She then spent 12 years working on sexuality education and HIV prevention for the UN, ActionAid and Marie Stopes.

But it was when she gave birth to her first child that she quickly "realized that there had been zero innovation in pelvic-floor health, even though 80% of expectant and new mums suffer with it in some way."

It was the inspiration behind what would become Elvie. "I didn't really have an idea for a company, I just thought there was a problem that needed to be solved and that tech could help," says Boler. She believed that tech could stimulate innovation and aid product design. Something she would then bring to market in equally new and innovative ways.

Boler's first action was to do her research into the best way to exercise pelvic floor muscles, but as she told *The Standard*, "This was done via a horrible device where women had to lie on their back in a hospital with a probe put in. I thought, 'Why can't we take the idea behind this thing that hospitals are using, and develop something fun and easy to use at home?' At the time, sports tech like Fitbit was launching, and I thought those kinds of sensors could be applied to women's health."

She pitched her idea to the government-backed Innovate UK scheme in 2013 and won a £100,000 grant. She quit her job to focus on making a better device: a Kegel trainer and app used to help women strengthen their pelvic floor via five-minute workouts involving games.

While working on early prototypes, she met Alex Asseily, the founder of wearable tech firm Jawbone, and he helped her change her mindset. "He came on board as a co-founder and investor, and encouraged me to take a Californian mentality, raising more money and hiring the 'A-team' of engineers."

It was two years before the £170 Elvie Trainer was launched. Already eschewing the traditional venues, Boler and her team hosted sales talks in west London and New York gyms and hosted parties in people's homes. It took a while for things to get going. "Eventually, it reached a tipping point via word-of-mouth success. Then all the retailers who'd thought we were crazy and said they weren't going to stock a vagina product began calling us back," says Boler.

After six months, the firm turned a profit; within a year, revenue hit $1 million then, three years after that launch, the Elvie Trainer was also made available on the NHS.

Riding on that success and the fame it got from being included in the $100,000 Oscars goodie bags and celebrity fans of the brand including Gwyneth Paltrow who featured it on her Goop site, Boler started planning her next product.

In 2017, Elvie raised £4.6 million from angel investors and started work on "the world's first silent wearable breast pump."

Its launch at the London Fashion Week saw Elvie's discreet pump peeping out of a black bra-wearing model mum. It was perfect demonstration that breast pumps didn't have to be loud and cumbersome.

The tactics obviously worked because, despite the £250 price tag, "it was an overnight success story," says Boler.

Turnover is now over £20 million and Elvie has been recognized as one of Wired's 'hottest start-ups' and one of the 15 start-ups 'To Watch' by *The Sunday Times*.

The brand and Boler's rise seems likely to continue. Elvie has four new femtech products in its R&D pipeline.

As Boler says, "Women tend not to talk about the health issues they're facing, despite the fact that they're completely normal. So by launching our products in a lifestyle space, we could normalize it.

"Until now, the tech industry has always thought that focusing on women customers means changing the colour of a product or turning it into a piece of jewellery. There's never been a tech brand for women before. That's our ambition."

A WOMAN'S
WORK

"I didn't get there by wishing for it or hoping for it, but by working for it."

ESTÉE LAUDER

Women work hard. They work well. They are committed and conscientious. They excel at multitasking and working with others. They are great team players and great team builders.

1. ASTHMA, ALLERGIES AND AN ALL-CONSUMING DRIVE FOR PERFECTION: THE RECIPE FOR SUCCESS

— MARGARET RUDKIN — PEPPERIDGE FARM

"My first loaf should have been sent to the Smithsonian Institution as a sample of Stone Age bread, for it was hard as a rock and about one-inch-high." So said Margaret Rudkin, the founder, original baker and driving force behind the Pepperidge Farm brand.

Margaret had started her career as a bank teller at McClure Jones and Co. in 1919. There she met Henry Rudkin, who she married in 1923. In 1926, the two purchased a property in Fairfield, built a home there and christened their estate 'Pepperidge Farm' after the pepperidge tree, Nyssa sylvatica, that grew locally.

Together they had three children, the youngest of whom was a sickly and asthmatic child. While this may not sound like a recipe for business success, it was to be the inspiration for the brand.

One of the biggest challenges Margaret faced was how to feed her child, whose severe allergies and asthma made him unable to eat most commercially processed foods. Taking the advice of a specialist, Margaret put him on a diet of fruits and vegetables and only minimal processed foods.

This meant that her son couldn't eat the commercially produced bread of the day, so Margaret decided to try baking him some more natural bread. She adapted a recipe from her grandmother and baked some stone-ground whole-wheat bread with the vitamins and nutrients intact.

Her first attempts could have put her off, but she persevered. "I started over again, and after a few more efforts by trial and error, we achieved what seemed like good bread."

Family and friends loved it but, more importantly, her son not only loved it, it helped improve his health. In fact, it helped so much that his doctor actually started 'prescribing' it to some of his other patients. Dr Donaldson even endorsed her bread, saying, "When Mrs Rudkin makes bread, she makes bread – the finest bread the world has ever known."

She decided to approach her local grocer and see if he would be willing to sell her Pepperidge Farm bread. He was sceptical at first but when she told him that she wanted her 'premium' bread to be sold for 25 cents, even though the going price for bread was 10 cents, he was even less convinced.

Margaret, however, calmly sliced up a loaf and gave him a taste and the proof of the pudding, or rather the bread, was in the eating. The grocer took all the loaves that she'd brought with her. When she got home, she was bursting to tell the family her good news, but it had beaten her there. The grocer had already called, leaving a message asking for more.

"Although I knew nothing of manufacturing, of marketing, of pricing or of making bread in quantities, with that phone call, Pepperidge Farm bread was born," Margaret later said.

Outgrowing her kitchen and then her garage, she helped design a state-of-the-art baking facility in Norwalk, Connecticut. On Independence Day, 4 July 1947, Margaret cut the ribbon, opening the facility.

While most of the bread-making process was automated, Margaret had insisted the bread was still kneaded by hand to ensure the final quality of the product.

With more success, the Rudkins were able to travel abroad, and it was on one of these trips that Margaret discovered a collection of fancy chocolate cookies produced by the purveyors to the Belgian Royal House. She secured production and distribution rights for Milano, Brussels and Bordeaux cookies, instinctively believing that other Americans would love them as much as she did.

Margaret led the purchase of Black Horse Pastry Company, foreseeing the growth of the home freezer market.

By the time Campbell Soup bought the company for about $28 million in 1961, Pepperidge Farm was selling more than $40 million worth of baked goods a year, up from about $3.5 million in 1950; the company had 1,500 employees working in six plants.

Margaret became the first woman to serve on the board of Campbell Soup.

Her trips to Europe continued and led to another opportunity. This time, she found a unique little fish-shaped cracker in Switzerland. The goldfish crackers were the creation of Oscar J. Kambly, who had wanted to make a snack for his wife. Her horoscope sign was Pisces, the symbol for which is a fish. Having decided on a fish, he chose the goldfish shape because it was a symbol of luck. It wasn't luck but Rudkin's good judgment that led her to taking them back to America, where they became and remain hugely successful.

In 1963, *The Margaret Rudkin Pepperidge Farm Cookbook* was published, containing a combination of her favourite recipes and memoirs. It was the first cookbook ever to make the bestseller list of *The New York Times*.

On 1 June 1967, Rudkin died of breast cancer. She had been an exceptional baker, a self-described perfectionist, and had been completely involved in the business from technological innovation to marketing strategies. She was an author and had for a while been the face of Pepperidge Farm in their television advertising. And if that wasn't enough, she still found time to guest-lecture at Harvard Business School.

Asked what made her company so successful, her answer was always the same: "My explanation for our extraordinary growth is that Pepperidge Farm products are the best of their kind in the world."

2. KEEPING HER HAND IN BY DESIGNING SOMETHING FOR HER FEET

– MARCIA KILGORE – FITFLOP

Marcia Kilgore has done a lot of different jobs in her life. She has been an aerobics instructor, a waitress, a gymnastics coach, a personal trainer. She has worked on a reception desk, done facials and waxing.

Oh yes, she has also founded, built and run five famous brands: Bliss, Soap & Glory, FitFlop, Soaper Duper and now Beauty Pie. And if that wasn't enough, she does the copywriting for all of them.

What follows is the story of one of those brands, FitFlop, but we could quite easily have written five stories.

Kilgore credits her entrepreneurial drive to the fact that her father died when she was just 13. "I took on three part-time jobs to help out my mother." One of those jobs included working in a gym, something that would play a big part in her future success.

At 18, she moved from her home in Canada to New York to attend Columbia University, a move that was to be funded by her elder sister, who was a model. Unfortunately, an unexpected and unexpectedly large tax bill for her sister meant her sister could no longer afford to give her any money.

She took a job in a New York gym but, having quickly decided the owner was useless, she left and became a personal trainer and, with a little help from her sister, she soon had a truly enviable client list, including the photographer Alex Chatelain, Carrie Fisher and Paul Simon.

It wasn't long before her entrepreneurial drive kicked in and, in 1996, she launched Bliss, the fashionable day spa, together with a range of beauty products. At this moment, her sister was to play another important role in her life. One of the products was a waxing kit that would be sold on QVC. Knowing she needed some help, her sister introduced her to Thierry Boué, a French consultant for Shiseido. Not only did Marcia hire him, she would later marry him and have two children with him. The couple also relocated to London when Thierry suggested moving back to Europe to be closer to his aging father.

In 2006, and, as she tells it, "mainly to keep her hand in," she dreamed up Soap & Glory, the mid-price range of cleaning and beauty products that's become one of Boots' bestsellers.

And she didn't stop there. Attending a conference and finding it a bit dull, her mind began to wander. She hit upon the idea of an unashamedly comfortable sandal. However, she instinctively understood that a stubby shoe that wasn't attractive was likely to struggle, and it would need to work hard to be loved.

Kilgore says she rarely wears heels but says, "I understand their appeal. Perhaps in the same way that texting has changed the way today's teenagers are using their fingers and ringing doorbells with their thumbs, some women may develop the muscles that allow them to wear heels nonstop.

But I wasn't one of them. My feet are too wide, I find them painful — and I don't like to be controlled by my shoes."

Thinking about that led to the other innovative twist Marcia conceived. She wanted the shoes "to be participative." Kilgore wondered if a shoe could deliver better-toned legs, but in a way that recognized that people believe that there is no gain without pain, or at least a little work!

"No one really believes that you can put on a cream that will make you thinner. They know you have to put in a bit of effort, but it has to be the kind of effort that's achievable. Everyone walks, so what if I could come up with a shoe that made their walk more effective?"

Excited by the idea, she started to explore how she could deliver the 'what if?' She interviewed a dozen shoe designers but discovered that shoe designers don't really know anything about the body.

She would have to find someone who might come at the problem differently so, on a visit to Swansea University, she sounded out the dean. He introduced her to his biomechanics department. "They immediately knew what I was talking about, but had no experience of shoe design."

Knowing what she now needed – biomechanics who knew something about shoes – she returned to London and eventually located her sole-mates (well, she does love a good pun, as Soap & Glory proves). Dr David Cook and Darren James were two biomechanics at London South Bank University, who knew about shoes and immediately 'got it.'

FitFlops, as the brand was called, were a blend of precision ergonomics under sporty-looking flip flop straps, but the fundamentals were the rules dictated by expert biomechanics. They created a revolutionary triple-density Microwobbleboard™, which was integrated into the WALKSTAR™ sandal, the first FitFlop product.

She and the brand try to be careful and not to overstate the FitFlop's properties and potential. "It's not a cure for cellulite," she qualifies, "but it can help tone you." The tagline on the advertising, which is another written by Marcia, was "the shoe with the built-in gym."

The brand has been a huge success, is available in 48 countries, and more than 10 million participative shoes have been sold.

While that's the end of this tale, Marcia's story continues with the more recent launch of Beauty Pie, a brand that *Forbes* describes as "ready to shake things up with a daring business model that brings beauty products directly to consumers without the exorbitant prices."

Clearly, Marcia is a lady for whom a woman's work is never done – there may be another idea just around the corner.

3. YOU CAN'T KEEP A GOOD GIRL DOWN

– SANDY LERNER – CISCO AND MUCH MORE

Sandy Lerner's entrepreneurial spirit first came to the fore to help her fund her education. Prior to going to college, she had spent some time at Clipper Gap ranch, and she bought a steer. A couple years later, she sold it for a healthy profit. She reinvested earnings, buying two more head of cattle. By the time she left for college, she had a herd of 30. Slowly selling them off provided an income stream that paid her college tuition.

She gained her bachelor's degree in political science in 1975. While she considered a career in academia, she felt her opportunities, especially financially, would be limited. She therefore went on to study for a master's degree in econometrics in 1977. It was while completing these studies that she discovered her interest in computer science. She was made manager of the computer lab and began to use the computers there to perform the data analysis she required for her degree.

She took her growing passion to Stanford. She gained her master's degree in statistics and computer science in 1981 and became the Director of Computer Facilities at Stanford Graduate School of Business. While working there, she met Leonard Bosack, who would later become her husband.

Sandy and Leonard's offices were pretty close, but they knew it would be much more convenient if they could share software and databases between them, other systems and other independent computers rather than relying on the time-consuming disk transfers that were the order of the day.

Using a router that Leonard had designed, they, together with a group of faculty members and some students, built and adapted it so that it was capable of connecting the computer systems between their offices. They built it further until the network spread across all of the systems throughout the school.

It was then that Sandy and Lerner realized that they were onto something big, and that something was Cisco Systems, Inc. So they both quit their jobs to focus on their new venture.

While there was growing demand, they had to learn how to run a business and things were seldom easy. Slowly, the business grew, and the contracts got bigger. After three years of hard work, they thought their luck was in when they finally received external funding from a venture capitalist named Donald Valentine.

He provided his own lawyer to draw up Sandy and Leonard's vesting agreement. With hindsight, the pair wish they had realized that, while this document included a clause about their founder's stock, it conveniently left out employment contracts. Shortly, they would discover that while the funds would benefit the company, the deal was to spell the end for them and Cisco.

Donald Valentine wasn't at all convinced at the way Lerner and her husband were managing the company and installed John Morgridge as CEO. Following numerous clashes with Sandy, Valentine used the lack of her employment contract as a means to fire her. Hearing this, Leonard showed his solidarity and resigned.

In another sad twist, the couple separated soon afterwards.

Better news was that both still had their stock options, which they started selling off, raising significant capital for both of them, running in the tens of millions of dollars.

For many people, this would have been a good time to retreat quietly into the background and live off the money she had earned. Not so for Sandy Lerner.

She has gone on to launch and be successful with an array of philanthropic, creative and business ventures. These included investing in the refurbishment of Chawton House, which was once owned by Jane Austen's brother, Edward Austen Knight, and where Austen wrote some of her books, publishing a sequel to Jane Austen's *Pride and Prejudice* titled *Second Impressions*, using the pen name of Ava Farmer and funding The Folsom Zoo in California, which is also known as the Misfit Zoo, as it cares for animals that have been deserted, abandoned or injured in the wild.

In the business world, she has co-founded another successful brand.

In 1990s pink, red and beige tones completely dominated the beauty industry palette. Wanting some real alternatives, Sandy decided that if the current cosmetic industry couldn't and wouldn't satisfy her tastes, she'd satisfy them herself. Her business manager, David Soward, introduced her to Wende Zomnir, who likewise wanted to shake things up. Together they co-founded Urban Decay, which was launched in January 1996 and offered ten lipsticks and 12 nail enamels, with colours inspired by the urban landscape and with names including Roach, Smog, Rust, Oil Slick and Acid Rain. Their first ad had a headline that asked provocatively, "Does Pink Make You Puke?"

The brand was a success and first sold to LVMH Moët Hennessy and then twice again before the current owner, L'Oréal, acquired it.

Sandy continues to be involved in a whole series of other ventures.

4. A STORYTELLER'S TALE: WHEN MADIBA MET SIMBA

– SANDY GRIFFITHS – SIMBA CRISPS (FRITO-LAY)

Some people are natural-born storytellers. One such storyteller is Sandy Griffiths, a South African by birth with a truly international career. We had the pleasure of interviewing her for this book (you can read this interview in the Insightful Interviews section of the book). She told us a number of stories, and this one really touched a chord. Rather than us retell it, we thought we would use the interview and let her tell it in her own words.

It is the story of how, when working for Simba Frito-Lay, she was lucky enough to meet and spend some time with one of her absolute role models – the man that all South Africans know, simply, as Madiba: Nelson Mandela.

"I was very blessed and privileged to spend a fair amount of time with the man.

"I don't know if I have ever told you this story. It was my first encounter with Mr Nelson Mandela. I had this friend – he did a mimic of Madiba – you would swear it was Nelson Mandela talking to you. A lot of South Africans can do that accent. He would mimic it to perfection.

"I was with Simba Crisps at the time. We had one of these night bells that would go off at night. It was quite late, and the bells went off. It was this friend – he had been bugging me all that week with his Mandela mimic. So when I heard this voice and it said, 'Hello, this is Nelson Mandela, I need to talk to your CEO,' I went, 'yeah, yeah, yeah' and put the phone down.

"Then the phone rang again, and it was the same guy – OK – at which point I said, 'Listen, I'm very stressed, just stop messing around with me. I will talk with you tomorrow. Don't call me back.' I put the phone down again – not realizing that I had put the phone down twice on Mr Nelson Mandela himself.

"His PA then called me, laughing – thank God. She said, 'Listen, Madiba actually called me twice. This is the real man,' and I thought thank God she was laughing.

"I said, 'Are you kidding me?'

"'No,' she said, 'Madiba wants to speak to your CEO.' I thought 'Oh my God!' I nearly passed out with fright. I thought I was going to get fired.

"So, I called the MD and said, 'I think I might have messed up big time.' He said, 'Oh no, what have you done now?' I said, 'I think I put the phone down on Madiba twice. He says he wants to talk to the CEO.' He said, 'WHAT?'

"Now I'm close to tears. So, all he says to me is, 'I don't know how you're going to do this, but go fix it.'

"So, I called the PA and told her the back-story and she said he [Madiba] actually thought it was funny because no one has ever put the phone down on him. But she said, 'You're going to pay for this.'

"Payment was that I got 'invited' the following morning to have breakfast with him. It was with a few other people in the industry. I soon learned just how clever Madiba was, first-hand, because what he had been calling the CEO for was to get our character – we had a character called Simba the lion that went to schools, where it was a big thing. He wanted the lion to show up with him at schools, because he was going there as part of the work that the Nelson Mandela Trust Foundation does. He wanted Simba the lion with him and free stock to give to the kids as part of a Christmas package.

"I had gone to breakfast with him that morning where I was a blubbering idiot; I had just sobbed to start with, but it was how I got to spend three weeks for two years with him, taking Simba the lion around and giving him free stock.

"And what I learned from that time with him – understanding the gentleness of the soul, the forgiving nature of that man – is that, after everything, there was no bitterness in him.

"He said to me, 'I can't poison the rest of my days by being bitter and twisted because my days are limited. I'm going to live my best life. I have no regrets because I did what was right at the time. I will continue doing what I think is right. If I regret what has happened to me all my life, I'm living history, I'm not living in the present.'

"For me, he's beyond iconic – he's just a man you felt greatness in the presence of, like I'd never felt before. So, if you took a role model who almost doesn't seem real in most people's eyes, it would be Madiba."

Footnote: Sandy has many more stories and if you get the chance to meet her and talk to her, ask her why her first words on meeting David Beckham were, "Are you trying to get me fired?" but how they went on to get on like a house on fire, or maybe ask her about the man working in "the music business" called Jon, whom she talked to for two hours before discovering who he really was.

5. AN UNCOMFORTABLE SILENCE

– EDWINA DUNN – DUNNHUMBY

You're a relatively new company employing 30 people and you've been invited to give a presentation to the board of directors at Tesco, one of the largest retailers in the UK.

While you're confident in what you're going to say, you know how important it is for the future of your business.

You finish your presentation and are met with …

Silence.

A silence that lasts a minute, a minute that feels like the longest 60 seconds of your life.

Finally, the then chairman, Lord MacLaurin, speaks.

He says, "What scares me about this is that you know more about my customers after three months than I know after 30 years."

Edwina Dunn and her husband and business partner Clive Humby broke into smiles. This was the beginning of not only a long-lasting relationship, but one that would transform the retail market.

Looking back on it, Ms Dunn says, "It was the defining moment."

What the presentation had done was demonstrate that, with their skills and software, they could do something the supermarket group hadn't been able to do for itself. They had shown how, using Tesco's own data, they could work out exactly what Tesco's customers were buying.

It would allow Tesco to launch their Clubcard and help ensure it was a huge success.

After a successful trial, the Clubcard was launched nationally and was an immediate hit with Tesco's customers. Millions of them signed up, tempted by the promise of money-off coupons and the special offers that had been arranged with the likes of Coca-Cola and Nestlé.

A year or two later, it enabled Tesco to overtake Sainsbury's and become the UK's largest retailer.

dunnhumby, as their business was called, was set up in 1990 and was a real partnership. Humby was the software and data expert, and Dunn was the chief executive and business and relationship manager who managed the day-to-day running of the business.

It was one of the first companies in the UK founded on data-led technology, analysing data to identify and predict consumers' spending patterns. It built on work the couple had previously done while they were both employed at the UK arm of an American software business, where, coincidentally, they had first met. They had married a year later.

Their first client had been the UK food wholesaler Booker, where they identified the value in the company's data and then mined it to help them improve factors such as distribution.

"The thing to remember is that data was thrown away in those days ... there was no such thing as data mining or data profiling, this was all new," says Ms Dunn.

On the back of this success, they were asked by a Tesco executive who had heard of their work and wondered if they might be able to help Tesco.

"They were struggling with their pilot, there was just so much data that they couldn't manage it," says Ms Dunn. "Remember that computers were not what they are today.

So, we were invited in to look at their data, and told not to get too excited, as it would only be one-off."

What dunnhumby did was to think differently about the challenge. Dunn remembers, "We brought in a statistician's mindset, which was 'some of the data, some of the time.' That is what the technology people at the time didn't grasp."

They didn't try to analyse all of the data; instead they used a 10% sample and showed how they could achieve between 95% and 99% accuracy. It was this approach and the results it had provided that had stunned the Tesco board.

Immediately following the meeting, Tesco and dunnhumby signed an agreement.

Sixteen years later, in 2010, Ms Dunn and Mr Humby sold the business to Tesco.

Ms Dunn says, "It had always been our intention to ultimately exit the business, and we had come to the end of our business plan. We had exceeded our numbers, and Tesco settled the debt fairly and squarely, no quibbles!

"They were happy, and we were happy. And we were tired, actually … I just needed a rest."

They rested for 12 months, but since then have gone back to work in other ventures including two nonprofit organizations: The Female Lead, which celebrates women's achievements, and Your Life, Future Finder, which seeks to encourage education of both science and maths subjects in schools. They also invest and support a new data intelligence company, Starcount, and Dunn sits on two Government Advisory Boards: Centre for Data Ethics and Innovation and GeoSpatial Commission

Footnote: Edwina Dunn was kind enough not only to let us tell her story, but to agree to an interview and to write a foreword so you can read more about her and her thoughts in those sections.

6. **SHE'S STILL STANDING**

– MARTHA LANE FOX – LASTMINUTE.COM AND MORE

Martha Lane Fox was a privileged young girl. She is the daughter of the eminent historian and *Financial Times* gardening columnist Robin Lane Fox. She went to Westminster School before going on to study at Oxford University. However, she isn't apologetic about it and doesn't try and hide the truth.

She did become a successful businesswoman, teaming up with Brent Hoberman in the 1990s to first raise the money for, and then launch, Lastminute.com. It was a tough challenge. Both in their 20s, they were some of the pioneers who blew the first internet bubble. Hoberman recalled a former boss of his saying, "How many under-30-year-olds have you met who have raised a million dollars off the back of a business plan?"

But then came the hard work. The pair attended endless networking events and numerous conferences (as it was a time before there was social media!). After a few months, they'd generated a media storm, and they got the investment they needed.

Martha became the face of everything people loved and hated about new dot-com technology. However, the attention she got sometimes at the expense of Hoberman wasn't of her choosing. "Back then, it was mortifying for me, and it still is, that anybody supposes I jumped in front of Brent. What upset me more than anything was photographs of us with him cut out."

She believes her role was important, but is the first to credit Hoberman. "We built Lastminute.com together, but it was 100% his idea."

Looking back, Hoberman is very philosophical about it all: "You don't expect to have a front-page newspaper story for a business that you're starting. I don't think either of us thought the PR side would catch fire like that, but I was obviously very happy when it did. She took a lot of rough with the smooth in that arena."

Hoberman always knew that this was one of her strengths. "People with real confidence have no arrogance; Martha knows that she has a commanding presence. When she speaks, she holds a room; you can hear a penny drop."

Lastminute.com launched in October 1998 and was an immediate success, and it was not long before they started adding offers on theatre tickets, DVD rentals and dating to the mix. It went from nothing to 500,000 regular users in just two years.

Martha explained that in the course of a few years she would become one of the few people to have lived through both a metaphorical and a literal crash. Lastminute.com had floated on the London Stock Exchange in March 2000 with a share price of 380p but that rose to an astronomical 511p by the end of the day.

Then came the first crash. The internet bubble burst and, six months after the IPO, the shares were worth only 80p. Martha bore the brunt of shareholders' anger. "A huge number of emails were sent direct to me. We had 135,000 individual shareholders, which is a relatively large number for quite a small company. In the month after the float, I probably got 3,500 to 4,000 pretty unpleasant emails. 'Bitch' was among the kinder comments."

However, as is often the case, the media furore the crash created and the talk of the collapse of the business wasn't a reflection of what was really happening in the business. The pair went on working hard to continue the brand's growth. There were, however, missteps along the way. Martha, who at the time was chief operations officer, says, "Without doubt, one of the worst days at Lastminute.com was when I had to make the whole customer service team redundant because we were going to outsource their role to India. In retrospect, that was probably a mistake."

Having helped see the business through the crisis, she decided she wanted a change and left Lastminute in November 2003. Despite some press speculation about her taking a senior role at Selfridges, she still hadn't taken a new job when crash number two happened.

In May 2004, while in Essaouira, Morocco, Martha was involved in a serious car crash. She was with her boyfriend, Chris Gorell Barnes, and visiting one of his friends when their car slipped on a treacherous road. Martha would spend two years in hospital, undergoing 23 operations. She now walks with a cane.

More positively in May 2005, Lastminute.com was sold and she received £13 million (a tidy sum, but not quite the £300 million some claimed).

In 2010, she took on the role of the UK's 'Digital Champion,' a government-endorsed role whose title she adapted from the less emphatic 'Digital Inclusion Champion.' It's a position she still occupies today.

She has other business interests too. She has been a member of the board of Marks & Spencer since 2007. She sits on the boards of Twitter, Donmar Warehouse and Chanel, and is a trustee of The Queens Commonwealth Trust. She entered the House of Lords as a crossbencher on 26 March 2013, becoming its youngest female member. She also has interest in prison reform and, in 2002, while still at Lastminute.com, she became a founding trustee of the human rights charity, Reprieve.

She's also co-founded the karaoke-bar chain Lucky Voice with Nick Thistleton while still in hospital in 2005. Karaoke is one of Martha many passions, and it is on record that her karaoke song of choice would be, appropriately, 'I'm Still Standing.'

7. FROM BAGS TO RICHES, THE REWARDS OF GREAT CUSTOMER SERVICE

– MICHELLE KERSHAW – LAKELAND

Alan Rayner founded Lakeland Poultry Packers, which sold agricultural plastics including covers for haystacks, silage sheeting, Lammacs – plastic coats to protect newborn lambs and what was the first indication of where the business would ultimately go – plastic bags for chickens.

In 1974, when Alan retired, his three sons, Sam, Martin and Julian Rayner, took over the business.

They had "a moment of inspiration [that] told us people who froze food also cooked it! So along came the 'Everything for Home Cooking' catalogue. We scaled down the agricultural side and headed in the direction of all things kitchenware."

It was to prove to be a great decision and the business blossomed.

Not long after the brothers took over the business, Michelle Kershaw joined them. She was completely customer-centric long before the term was first used. She quickly learned everything there was to know about home freezing and kitchenware and became their resident expert and the face of Lakeland.

She went on to become their customer director but, as Julian readily admits, "Michelle was Lakeland. She had a huge personality, huge confidence. You couldn't replace her. If something wasn't right, you knew about it from Michelle. She would speak up for the customer."

Never much of a cook, Michelle had a passion for cleaning. Every Friday, she would take home a bag full of products and test them over the weekend. If she thought something was 'crap,' she would say so, but if it did its job, she wanted to tell her customers.

Michelle would always be in the office at 7am brewing a litre of coffee. "She never looked less than perfect and had a room the same size as her bedroom full of glitzy clothes," says her PA, Barbara Shepherd. "You had to be careful about admiring anything because she would give it to you – she was that generous."

Lakeland customers were her 'friends.' They rang her when their dogs died, they came to visit her in Windermere and sent cards. If they found a wonderful product on holiday, they couldn't wait to get back and tell her – the soft liquorice from Australia that is selling by the ton started as a customer suggestion. This meant that the company didn't, and doesn't, need to conduct formal market research, as it talks and listens to its customers on the phone, constantly.

Michelle was diagnosed with lung cancer in March 2003 yet, despite her illness, she continued working long hours. She was told that she needn't and shouldn't come in before 8.30am, but she came in early as always. Later that year, she was given the Lifetime Achievement Award for services to the home shopping industry.

On the day before she died in 2004, Michelle was driven to the office in the afternoon. Too weak to get out of the car, she checked proofs in the car park. Next morning, her last act was to finish a customer letter. When told of her death, there was a huge, heartfelt outpouring of grief from customers.

8. THE BEAR NECESSITIES OF BUILDING A BRAND

– MAXINE CLARK – BUILD-A-BEAR

Maxine Clark has always liked shopping, and in an interview with *Fortune* in 2015 she recalls, "One of my favourite things as a child was to go shopping with my mom and looking was as good as buying. I always had a curiosity about how people shopped."

So, perhaps it was no surprise that, when she graduated from college, she went to work in the retail industry. More of a surprise is that having reached the upper levels of the industry, becoming president of ShoeSource, she found herself dissatisfied. "When I got to the top, my financial rewards were very high, but my psychic income bank account was nearly empty. I felt the retail world had lost its spark. I wanted to be more creative again, so, in 1996, I left the company."

Maxine, however, kept on shopping and was just as curious as she had been as a child and, as she told *Fortune*, "One day, I was shopping with Katie Burkhardt, the daughter of one of my good friends, and her brother Jack, who collected Ty Beanie Babies. When we couldn't find anything new,

Katie picked up a Beanie Baby and said we could make one. She meant we could go home and make the small bears, but I heard something different. Her words gave me the idea to create a company that would allow people to create their own customized stuffed animals. I did some research and began putting together a plan."

The plan was for an interactive retail destination where kids could make personalized furry friends. With her experience as a buyer, she knew how things were made and how she could source the components. She knew about siting and how to run a retail operation.

However, when she started to talk to her potential audience, friends who were mothers and fathers, it seemed like there might be a problem. Those first parents she spoke to kept saying things like, "Why would anyone want to make your own stuffed animal when you can buy it at Target?"

Luckily, or perhaps just sensibly, she also spoke to the kids of those friends and their response was the polar opposite. They were excited by the idea of getting the chance to do it for themselves. It was at this point that Maxine decided that she needed a Cub Advisory Board, a group of children who offer their opinions about the products and services. As Maxine says, "Kids have insights and offer inspiration by looking at the world differently."

Convinced she was really onto something, in 1997, Maxine withdrew $750,000 from her retirement account to get the now-named Build-a-Bear Workshop going. The money would cover start-up costs and the building of the first prototype store. She also secured a bank line of credit for inventory and working capital, with her house as collateral.

Even that wasn't enough, as Maxine knew from the start that she wanted more. "I knew I wanted to build a multimillion-dollar business with hundreds of units, and I realized

I didn't have the ready cash to fund that growth. I knew I'd have to partner with outside investors."

Maxine went looking for PR opportunities and when 'coming soon' signs prompted a St. Louis business journal to run a story about the first store and its unique hands-on approach, it was seen by Barney Ebsworth, who owned a private investment firm. Ebsworth and his business partner, Wayne Smith, believed in the idea and bought in at 20% for $4.5 million, providing sufficient capital for several years.

The first store opened in the St. Louis Galleria on a Sunday and – always a good sign – there were lines out the door.

Despite early resistance from some mall landlords, who didn't at first 'get' the concept, its success soon had them begging Maxine and her team to come on in. Other investors noticed the success, too, and more funds came in. "We had to turn investors away after that because the business was so successful, we didn't need their money," says Maxine.

The original offer was just bears and clothes, but the range soon expanded to include shoes and accessories, and then more animals. They moved into licensing products, carrying costumes from Disney and Major League Baseball teams.

Looking back, Maxine recognizes that, "At a time when everything was going high tech, high touch and hands-on was a good balance."

However, Build-a-Bear also harness technology to good effect. "We started when the internet was just getting popular, so we were able to track people in our loyalty program from day one, and continually do customer research. We're constantly creating new products, so there's no niche that needs to be filled. Everything is focused on the customers and giving them a good experience."

Build-a-Bear also wanted to give something back, long before the notion of brand purpose became popular.

As Maxine explains, "We want to engage kids beyond selling them something in our store. Every year, we look for ten children around the country who are doing things to help their communities, and we name them our Huggable Heroes."

In 2004, they opened their first overseas store in Japan and are now in 19 countries.

In June 2013, Maxine stepped down from her Chief Executive Bear role to apply her entrepreneurial skills to her passion for improving K-12 public education and to invest in and mentor women and minority entrepreneurs.

Footnote: *if you want to know more about Maxine and her story, she published her first book,* The Bear Necessities of Business: Building a Company with Heart, *in 2006.*

9. HELPING OTHERS

– MARGARET MOLLOY – WEARINGIRISH

Ishbel Maria Hamilton-Gordon, Marchioness of Aberdeen and Temair, 1857–1939, known more simply as Lady Aberdeen, was a Scottish author, philanthropist and an early advocate of woman's interests. Her husband, Lord Aberdeen, was Lord Lieutenant of Ireland for a short period in 1886.

She helped organize a special Irish craft exhibit at the World's Columbian Exposition in Chicago in 1893, which featured a selection of Irish crafts and crafts workers, including 40 young Irish craftswomen. Its success led to the establishment of a depot for the Irish Industries Association in Chicago. Lady Aberdeen went on to help establish Irish lace schools across the island to help women develop a craft in what were financially unstable times.

Now some 125 years later, another famous woman is championing the skills of Irish designers and this is her story and the story of WearingIrish.

Margaret Molloy is global chief marketing officer at Siegel+Gale, the strategic branding and design consultancy.

Unlike Lady Aberdeen, she has worked her way up through the ranks. She grew up on a dairy farm in Ireland, where she learned that "hard work will set you free." Her first job was with an Irish organization in the US, for which she left Ireland for New York City.

Her ensuing career was in client-side marketing roles at technology and services companies. She attributes her success to a combination of three things: "credentials, networks and external validations."

"I always made sure I have credentials to do the job I am being assigned; for example, I did my graduate work with the Harvard Business School – that's a powerful credential. I also build external networks, particularly among clients, which gives me a level of influence and authority. I also have a high public profile, which provides external validation outside my direct role. These elements have helped me overcome any obstacles that may exist."

She joined Siegel+Gale in 2013. However, Molloy has never forgotten her Irish heritage, and despite the immense pressure on her time and diary, she regularly finds time to meet with new people, especially the young Irish who were looking for help in their careers.

She will listen to them, give them advice and often provide them with a relevant contact with whom they can connect. It continues a tradition of the Irish helping their own settle and succeed in a new world.

Her commitment to helping young Irish people was to take a step further one March, which is known as Irish American heritage month in the US. She attended an Irish American heritage event and was struck by the outfit of a prominent Irish American woman. She asked her what or rather 'who' she was wearing. Margaret was surprised and perhaps a little disappointed to hear it was all continental European and American designers. Molloy immediately saw that this had been a missed opportunity to showcase the flair and creativity of Irish fashion. This realization was to be the spur for WearingIrish.

"As the creator of WearingIrish, I help Irish fashion designers tell their stories. And in so doing, my vision is to uplift all Irish industry, business and talent by positioning Ireland as a creative nation."

She harnesses her marketing skills to help achieve this vision, noting, "We're in a moment where people are desirous of connecting with brands that speak to them – brands that have a story to tell. Ireland is filled with designers that do exactly that: create products brimming with provenance, authenticity and quality."

In summer 2018, WearingIrish brought over a group of Irish fashion designers to share their goods and stories with the American market. The results were positive and, in the case of designer Alison Conneely, immediate, as her designs were taken up by Bloomingdale's. Other designers have also found American patrons and are negotiating deals.

In January 2019, and taking us back to the beginning of this story, WearingIrish hosted a screening of *Snáithe*, the story of Irish fashion in which, among other things, the tale of Lady Aberdeen is told.

10. GUERRILLA GARDENING: PLANT WHEREVER YOU LIKE

– MARY CLEAR AND PAM WAKEHURST
– INCREDIBLE EDIBLE

In 2008, Pam and Mary met with a group of friends in a local café to talk about what they could do to encourage people to think differently about the power and potential of their future. The question they asked themselves was, "Can we find a unifying language that cuts across age, income and culture that will help people themselves find a new way of living, see spaces differently, think about the resources they use differently, and interact differently?"

The answer was food, which would subsequently be translated into their all embracive mantra of "if you eat, you're in."

The first result was a seed swap among the friends to encourage people to grow their own produce. Then, Mary lowered one of the walls in her front garden, removing rose bushes to make a bed with herbs and put up signs saying, "Help yourself."

This spurred the group on to think bigger – what if they took over unloved places, planted vegetables in them and encouraged people to take what they needed? Not only did they think bigger, they started to act bigger too. They weren't believers in strategy documents or applying for grants. They believed in the power of small actions. They believed in making things happen, and without the complication and potential delays that would have been caused by asking permission. They felt it would be easier to ask forgiveness than permission.

"You can do nothing and obey the rules, or you can say 'I'm going to make a difference regardless.' And, you know, the prisons are full. They've got enough on without getting a load of grannies for cleaning up," says Clear.

The first 'unloved' patch they adopted and adapted was a local grass verge, which Pam says, "previously seemed to attract only dog poo." It was turned into a herb garden.

Signs were nailed to walls around town without permission from the council, benches emblazoned with their logo were installed without asking. Even some beds outside the police station were put together and maintained without formal permission.

While not keen on waiting for permission, they did start to build relationships with business owners, educators, local government officials and community members.

At the heart of Incredible Edible is what Pam and Mary call the three-plate model of society: community, education and business. The aim is to have all of the plates spin together around food, and thus have food inevitably become a part of all aspects of society.

So, having started to engage the community, they spread into education, partnering with a local high school and helping create an aquaponics system and orchard for students to participate in farming fish and growing fruit and vegetables. The project would have such success that the school added agriculture to the curriculum and acquired a plot of land to use as a market garden training centre.

To help local business Incredible Edible developed a scheme so that locally sourced products in stores could be badged with the Incredible Edible's logo, as the brand could easily be recognized. The result was that 49% of the stores that traded Incredible Edible food saw an increase in profits.

Pam sums this up, saying, "We have been planting up our public realm – and please note the word public – with things we can eat, to demonstrate what we can all grow for ourselves in our front and back gardens. We have been getting teachers to understand the importance of putting local food right at the heart of the curriculum, whatever the subject. And we have been supporting our local food market and small shops through the power of the pound in our pockets.

"It's not rocket science, but it means we all have a chance to be part of tomorrow's solutions, not problems."

Today, there are growing spaces all around Todmorden: garden plots dot the town's streets; corn stalks stretch tall in front of the police station; the land around the local hospital and health centres is bursting with produce that has replaced the previous prickly plants and even the cemeteries host raised beds full of collard greens and cabbage.

Incredible Edible's vision to create kind, confident and connected communities through the power of food has started to spread, helped by a TED talk by Pam that has now been viewed more than three quarters of a million times. Projects are popping up everywhere. There are over 100 groups in towns in the UK and some 500 community-food growing groups across the world using the Incredible Edible name.

Writing an opinion piece in *The Guardian* in 2014, Pam is on record as saying, "The most amazing thing is the response of our local authority and other far-sighted councils across the UK. They know they don't have the maintenance budgets they once did. So what's better than to encourage citizens to grow food across the public realm, or putting all spare land on a website so people can see where they can grow near to their homes, or setting up a licence so people know the rules? Or getting staff to support their residents in making their town more edible and, by doing so, improving relations, getting people more active and encouraging people to just get on and show a little initiative in their own town."

One of Mary's favourite memories is a meeting with royalty. For someone who grew up in absolute poverty and had to deal with being ostracised because she was one of a family of five illegitimate children, meeting Prince Charles meant a lot to her. He told her that he shares the belief that food can be used to be kind to others and promised her that "When I'm king, you can plant wherever you like."

So, with or without your permission, you better get ready for more "guerrilla gardening."

INSIGHTFUL INTERVIEWS

THE INTERVIEWS – WHO'S WHO

What follows are edited highlights from a series of interviews we did with some of the amazing women in marketing today. They include some well-known names together with women you will never have heard of. This is by design. We talked to a broad age range to illustrate the changes over the decades; women who started their careers in the 1970s–1980s, through to the 1990s–2000s, through to Millennials to understand the differences in the 21st century world. They come from a mix of sectors from FMCG (fast-moving consumer goods) and retail to financial service, travel and pharma. They represent a range of specialisms from marketing director roles, to chief customer officer and PR. Many have vast international experience, so you can be inspired by stories from the UK as well as Europe, Asia, Africa and the US.

We took a qualitative approach to their stories, talking to them for one hour about why they chose marketing as a career, interesting stories around their experiences, what it's like being a woman in marketing, the challenges they have faced as a woman, what unique benefits women bring to marketing and their role models.

We have structured the interviews around the years that our Wonder Women started their careers, alongside waves of feminism. We hope this will enable the reader to observe similarities and differences and identify where changes have occurred and where there is still much work to be done.

1970s–1980s: WOMEN'S LIB

- Edwina Dunn
- Henrietta Jowitt
- Helle Muller Petersen
- Pat Taylor
- Sarah Henwood
- Elaine Barnes
- Catherine Querné

1990s–2000s: GIRL POWER

- Gemma Greaves
- Kara McCartney
- Kate Thornton
- Kathy Leech
- Sandy Griffiths
- Elena Marchenko
- Harriet de Swiet
- Sally Bibb
- Catherine Grainger

2012–THE PRESENT (MILLENNIALS): HASHTAG ACTIVISM

- Jossie Morrison
- Rebecca Lury
- Lottie Unwin

1970s–1980s
WOMEN'S LIB

These Wonder Women grew in the 60s and 70s and entered their careers in the 70s and 80s amid the second wave of feminism. Whereas the first wave began with the suffragettes and the focus on achieving the right to vote, the second wave was all about full equality: equal rights in the workforce, sexual liberation (and access to the Pill and abortion) and freedom from intimidation and violence. Women now sought to achieve this equality through opportunities in education and a career beyond their homes.

Our Wonder Women working in the UK experienced the first female Prime Minister, the formidable Margaret Thatcher. Although she's often criticized for her failure to either promote 'women's issues' or to improve women's political representation, the 1980s became an era where "anything was possible." Women's share of professional jobs increased, and they moved into management roles.

EDWINA DUNN

Edwina D. Dunn, OBE, is an entrepreneur in the field of data science and customer-centric business strategy. Edwina and her husband, Clive Humby, founded dunnhumby, the global leader in customer data science, which was central to the success of the Tesco Clubcard. You can read our take in the earlier story, "An Uncomfortable Silence" on page 131.

During the interview, we discussed her rise to success, the importance of company culture, loyalty, knowing customers better than anyone else, having big ideas, how trying and failing is liberating, the power of two, resilience, proving people wrong, her Female Lead project and why it's OK for women to be ambitious.

DID YOU PLAN YOUR CAREER IN MARKETING?

I was a geographer. I never thought anything I studied was going to help me in a job. I just landed in an exceptionally good place. My first job was an extraordinarily entrepreneurial company – I had a P&L (profit & loss statement responsibility) from the age of 24, I suddenly became responsible for hiring people and a sales line. It was a fantastic culture – you could determine what you wanted to do and how far you wanted to go.

It was a company that taught you how to run a business. It was as simple as that. Then, of course, you can't put the genie back in the bottle. Once you've learned how to run a business, when you see the next opportunity, you go for it.

I remember looking up the definition of marketing and thinking, "Gosh, that is exciting – it's all about understanding, anticipating and satisfying customer needs profitably." So that became my mission – to know customers better than anyone else.

WHAT LED TO YOUR SUCCESS?

When Clive and I founded dunnhumby, people were throwing data away because it was too expensive to store. There weren't any models to rely on. It was unknown territory. We were creating it as we went along, using the logic of data. It was highly creative and stimulating.

At the time, 20 years ago, all the data on customer transactions was bigger than all of the computers at the time and a terabyte of data cost $1m. Now, a terabyte is about $15.

With previous experience in what is now called geospatial analysis, we were pushing the very edge of what could be done, and that gave us the big break. We were given a job by Tesco because their IT department couldn't crack it.

We broke the rules everyone else was playing by. We didn't try to analyse all of the data all the time – we did some of the data some of the time.

WHAT DROVE YOU ON?

The wonderful thing about entrepreneurship is you learn not to be fearful of what's never been done. Trying and failing is part of the process and is very liberating.

The 1980s was an era when you were told politically, "You can be more, you can go out there and make a business, make money." Everything just led us to believe we could do anything we wanted as long as we worked hard enough – and we did work incredibility hard. I think that's the pattern of anybody who wants to make a difference.

We were also lucky because Tesco were phenomenal executers. We delivered the insights and the plan; they didn't hesitate – they did it. To this day, I haven't seen many companies like them.

AT WHAT POINT DID YOU DECIDE TO EXPAND?

We thought we could either be a big fish in a small pond and never grow or find a way to get into a much bigger pond, like America.

We worked out a strategy, which had three phases.

First, helping Tesco outperform their competitors.

Second, repurposing the data for Tesco's suppliers, the manufacturers, then selling them media, e.g., coupons, mailings and posters to advertisers. This second phase was transformational. We started selling all of the Tesco data, with their permission – anonymized – to the manufacturers.

We then realized that CPGs (consumer packaged goods) are global, where retailers aren't. So, it was fine to be in the UK just with Tesco, but if we were going to work with Coca-Cola or Kraft or General Foods, we had to be in about 12 markets where most consumers bought these big billion-dollar brands. So, that became the third phase of the new strategy.

We went to America, then, literally to every country around the world and said, "We're going to work here, we're going to work with one of the top three retailers, would you like it to be you?"

But the grocery retailers weren't used to working with consultancies, so we had to create a model that ticked all the boxes for them, and this is what we proposed:

- A joint venture model in which half of our resources were dedicated to making them number one, as we have done with Tesco in the UK – TICK

- They give us all their data, we sell it to all of their suppliers and they give us that exclusively – TICK
- In return, we will give them half of the joint venture – TICK

We decided that half of a big pie was better than the whole of the small pie.

As soon as we did that, they never let us fail. Whatever help we needed, whatever voice we needed, guidance, connections – they were truly invested. For them, it was sense of partial control, it paid for the work we did, they didn't feel they were being fleeced by a consultancy.

It built a mutual trust. Once we had retailers in about 25 countries, then the CPGs would use us everywhere in the world and, suddenly, it became a global language.

IT'S AN AMAZING STORY. LOOKING BACK, WHAT ARE YOU MOST PROUD OF?

Everybody told us it won't work, you're going to fail in America – everyone fails in America – but we didn't fail. We built a business from scratch; it grew to about $1 billion in revenue and was hugely profitable.

We also built a team of the best people. People I liked, respected and admired. They've gone on to do amazing things.

We made money, we made our clients and partners money, our employees made money and customers loved the loyalty rewards – it was win/win/win. And we absolutely loved what we were doing – you can't do it for 20 years and not love it.

BEING A WOMAN IN MARKETING AND BUSINESS, YOU HAVE TO BE ENORMOUSLY RESILIENT AND ENERGETIC.

— EDWINA DUNN

TELL US ABOUT THE POWER OF TWO. IS IT THE COMBINATION OF YOU AND CLIVE WORKING TOGETHER, COMBINING MALE/FEMALE CHARACTERISTICS, OR IS IT MORE THAN THAT?

When you marry an opposite and work together, you have someone you can rely on and trust, but you also get a different perspective. You stick together through thick and thin, you survive the tough bits, you have fun when it's great, you enjoy the spoils when everything works out, but it does have to be equally involving and fulfilling for both of you.

We used this idea of sending people in pairs for jobs – they were not best buddies, and more likely to be people with different skills. They either survived, thrived or killed each other! Fortunately, they mostly thrived. When the pairs talked about it afterwards, they would say it was the hardest thing they have ever done, but never in their career, before or since, have they grown so much. They realized they had the power to do anything they set their eyes on – if they did it together.

I'm a huge believer in not working alone. When you work with someone who's exactly the opposite, then you never have to worry about all the things you're bad at. Clive is good at everything that I'm bad at: he's a computer scientist, a mathematician, he understands how businesses work inside and out, but he used to say, "I don't really want to talk to anybody – you do the commercial stuff, it doesn't interest me."

WHAT HAVE BEEN THE CHALLENGES AS A WOMAN IN MARKETING?

We often used to laugh. We were working with retailers and financial advisors who were all male. My favourite card features a Punch cartoon, where they say, "That's very good Miss Tiggs, now if one of the men would like to make the same point, we can all move on."

It was honestly like that. I'd say something, and everyone would look slightly perplexed, then Clive would say it, and everyone would say, "Oh yes, great idea." It was a source of amusement. If you don't laugh about something, you cry.

Being a woman in marketing and business, you have to be enormously resilient and energetic. I had a great motivation – the more people told me I couldn't, the more determined I was to show them. Maybe it's a stubborn streak in me.

Oprah Winfrey said that in an interview: "The reason I'm so rich is that the studios said that I wouldn't build the audience to the size I did – so I negotiated a huge percentage. That's what's made me successful – everyone predicted I would fail."

CAN YOU TELL US ABOUT YOUR FEMALE LEAD PROJECT?

When we sold the business, we made more money than we ever dreamed of – which I hope doesn't sound arrogant – it was beyond my expectations, but I recognized that it came with responsibility. I wanted to help others, other women in particular. The Female Lead is part of that. Its aim is to provide positive role models for future generations, nurturing young women's confidence and ambition in all spheres.

The book has stories of 60 inspirational women from many walks of life. It's a celebration of women's achievements, endeavours and diversity.

Now we've got the book, a website, and video films. We've created a Female Lead Society. We're in 7,000 schools in the UK, and even more in the US. We've done groundbreaking research into the untapped potential of social media to enhance teen aspiration and promote positive mental health. Our DisruptYourFeed Campaign proved that you can detoxify social media for young girls and reveal to them a world of excitement and empowerment.

AND GOING FORWARD?

We want to encourage the positives and reduce the harms of social media and workplace politics – to build resilience in girls and women.

I'm really proud of all that I am and have done, and I happen to be female. We have lots of conversations around what is feminism – the answers you get are so varied. The tipping point now is to make sure we keep the positivity and the balance, because the momentum is there.

Girls are wary of the words 'ambition' and 'role models' – there's still a concern it's unfeminine or prescriptive. They will talk about 'passion' and 'women who inspire.' We just need to say – it's OK to be ambitious but that there are many types of fulfilment, not just money and power.

I remember going to get career advice and being told, "You will be a nurse, a teacher or a secretary."

My response was, "Really? Will I?"

HENRIETTA JOWITT

Henrietta is Deputy Director General – Commercial at the CBI. She started her career as a graduate working on Heinz Baked Beans, then progressed in FMCG brand-led organizations before switching to the very different world of professional and financial services.

During our interview, we talked about what it was like to be a woman in marketing in the 1980s, how women are good at building teams, communicating, seeing the bigger picture, and harnessing their EQ and intuition to develop great understanding, insight and ideas.

WHY DID YOU CHOOSE A CAREER IN MARKETING?

I knew I wanted to go into business but wasn't sure what discipline. After attending a course on business at university, I identified either finance or marketing as central to driving business forward – so I narrowed my choice to those two. I had friends in accountancy, but what they were doing sounded dull and boring – counting dinner jackets in a warehouse as part of an audit! So, I chose marketing.

I was the first female graduate that Heinz UK hired in marketing and started on an iconic product, Baked Beans. I ended up as product manager for pasta, then decided I wanted a broader perspective, so spent some time working at a small advertising agency before going back 'client-side,' taking on the role of marketing manager at Nestlé, working on Smarties and Kit-Kat in York.

WHAT WAS IT LIKE IN MARKETING IN THE 1980S?

It was fun, intellectually challenging and exciting, a good balance of responsibility across commerce and creativity. The 1980s were a good time to be in marketing, but there were challenges as a woman in business and sometimes you just had to 'suck it up.' I remember incidents of sexism in the workplace that made me feel uncomfortable, but they seemed to be the norm so were difficult to challenge.

At Heinz, we had to learn about all parts of the business, from manufacturing to finance and law, but when it came to it, they weren't sure I should be allowed to be a sales rep because it wouldn't be safe. The notion of me in a Morris Marina with a boot full of beans as dangerous or that I would be in danger was frankly ridiculous, but it was the prevailing culture at the time. In the end, I duly went out as a rep and did a good job. Maybe they were concerned about my welfare because all the other reps were blokes.

At other times it was more blatant. I went on a training course run by the advertising agency, where I was the only woman. At the end, all the attendees had to make a presentation that was filmed. When it was played back to review, the footage of me stood out. All the other presenters had classic head and shoulders shots, but when I was presenting the camera spent most its time going up and down my legs. The head of the agency was incredibly embarrassed and made a point of apologizing to me. He was so impressed by my actual contribution that he offered me a job.

There was another occasion when I was working in a small agency. One evening, all the secretaries had gone home at 6pm and suddenly a call came in and we had to rush something out. The MD asked me if I could type the response. He just expected me to be able to type because that's what all women were taught, weren't they! Well, I had deliberately not learned to type for precisely that reason, and anyway they did not offer that course at Oxford when reading natural sciences.

However, as I became more senior at other brand-led FMCG companies such as Nestlé and United Biscuits, where marketing had a greater role in driving the business, I was well respected, and these sorts of things happened less and less. Times and attitudes changed.

Things have definitely improved, but there's still more to do. Most of the misogynistic behaviour has thankfully been eradicated, but becoming a parent, flexible working and pay and promotion to senior roles are still areas that need real focus to be truly fair and inclusive for women in business.

YOU THEN MOVED INTO MARKETING IN PROFESSIONAL AND FINANCIAL SERVICE ORGANIZATIONS. HOW DID YOU FIND THE TRANSITION?

It was very different outside of FMCG. I was shocked and dismayed to discover that marketing wasn't seen in the same light as in FMCG companies. For many people in professional and financial services, marketing was seen as "organizing events and colouring things in." They had little understanding of business strategy, planning, understanding your customers or clients, and orientating your business to meet their needs profitably.

I suppose this was more a lack of knowledge about – and therefore a prejudice against – marketing rather than women. Marketing just wasn't valued, did not hold the P&L and drive the business strategy, and too often advice and business recommendations were ignored or not taken seriously.

GIVE THEM WINGS AND TEACH THEM HOW TO FLY.

– HENRIETTA JOWITT

WHAT ARE YOU MOST PROUD OF?

I'm proud of my ability to build teams and help develop and encourage colleagues who have worked for me. In some ways, it's a bit like the experience of being a mum or parent where you want to help your child grow and develop. You need to allow them to be who they want to be, do what they are great at and will make them happy and thrive, and then you let go, give them wings and teach them how to fly.

I've worked with some great people, and seeing where they are now and what they have achieved makes me feel really proud to have played a small part in the development of their wings and flying skills.

WHAT IS IT THAT WOMEN ARE ESPECIALLY GOOD AT IN MARKETING?

That's a difficult question, because clearly it is not gender specific and it's a spectrum. Some men have what can be called feminine traits and some women have lots of so-called masculine traits.

However, I do think that women tend be good at empathizing with the customer's point of view – women instinctively 'get' what other women need and want. This is important because research shows that women influence over 80% of household expenditure – way beyond the grocery shop. Walking in your customers' shoes helps you to understand them better.

While not true of everyone, men focus on the details, the technicalities, what makes things work, where women are better at standing back and seeing the bigger picture. Men are more function and features led, whereas the best female marketers are concerned with understanding what their customers need, how to give it to them and make money from it.

Women are better at harnessing their EQ and intuition. It's not that data and analysis aren't really important and, as a scientist, I believe in them strongly. But women are open to how they 'feel' about something. I'm conscious that I say things like, "It doesn't feel right – I have a sense that something is missing." I rarely hear men saying this.

I think many women are good at building teams. It's not an exclusive trait but, on balance, they are generally better at it; they're better at involving and bringing people with them rather than directing and controlling; they are more open to being interested in the whole person, not just the job they're doing; they are inclined to collaborate, not compete.

Women are less likely to seek out the spotlight, to take the credit for the glory – they're more modest. They take their rewards in other ways – the feeling of a job well done, a shared success, having built a team or helped someone else to succeed.

AND WHAT ABOUT THE FUTURE?

I'm optimistic. Marketing has a critical role to play in building successful businesses. If you don't understand your customer and don't behave in a way that demonstrates empathy and service to society, then you will not build a successful business. While there is still more to do, we're moving in the right direction. The whole inclusivity agenda has caught up with business and different skills and approaches, especially leadership with high EQ as well as IQ now increasingly valued and good marketers have always led in that way.

The future lies in a balance of structure and creativity, of analysis and emotion, of diversity of thinking, and of each person in an organization feeling that they belong so that they can give of their best.

HELLE MULLER PETERSEN

Helle is now Country Director and SVP for Arla Denmark.

Previously, she had a long and successful career at Carlsberg, where her last role was managing director of the Carlsberg Croatia Group – the only female country MD within the Group.

Hailing from Denmark, her roles have given her a truly international perspective, with postings in six countries as well as working across more than 80 markets (in WE/EE and Asia). At Carlsberg, she was best known as 'the fairy godmother of Tuborg,' helping drive the success of the brand, resulting in it becoming larger than Carlsberg.

She is most passionate about building and leading teams, developing and nurturing talent.

WHY DID YOU DECIDE TO GO INTO MARKETING?

In Denmark, you intern for two weeks in a company when in grade seven or eight at school. My dad was a journalist and he explained to me why it was important to have advertising in a newspaper. I wanted to find out more about it, so I did my internship in a local advertising agency. I felt hugely empowered and this influenced my choice of what to study at university. I wanted something that was sufficiently broad enough to stimulate me but also had a commercial focus, so I decided to study business. I did a course with a language option, as I've always dreamt about having an international career.

While I was writing my thesis, Carlsberg was searching for international business trainees. I was called for an interview. I think what made me stand out was that I was the only one who came from a business school/university outside of Copenhagen – the only one in the room speaking with a heavy accent from Jutland.

WHAT KEY EVENTS SHAPED YOUR CAREER?

My first boss was not a marketer but was a good traditional sales guy. He told me to remember that although I have a master's degree, I must never forget that "a beer is something you drink, you enjoy and then you pee out." I've always remembered this – don't make it more fancy than it's supposed to be, don't take the fun out of it, don't make it so complicated that the sales guys don't know how to sell the story. He taught me to keep it simple.

The second thing is that I have red hair and am blessed with natural curls. When I started working in our international department, everybody there would come to the office wearing suits, socks that were sufficiently long enough so you couldn't see any skin. My first day in the office, my boss was standing at the elevator and asked me, "Are you doing gardening work today?" I wasn't smart enough to realize he was commenting on my dress. A couple years later, he asked me to make a presentation and I came up – big red curly hair – and he looked at me and said, "Just promise me one thing, Helle – don't let the dress code kill your personality." It taught me the importance of staying true to who I am. He gave me permission to be myself.

Another thing was taking the job in Kathmandu. I have always been willing to take chances. I think the real reason I became a CEO was because I was crazy enough to accept it – living with a family in Kathmandu is not on the top of most people's lists. There were candidates who were more experienced than me, who were men, but I was the crazy one who accepted it.

Lastly, my recent move to another great company (Arla Foods) has taught me the importance of 'owners' mentality.' Arla Foods is a farmer-owned cooperative and everything we do has a direct impact on the farmers and their families. You can't hide behind large PowerPoint presentations and Excel spreadsheets; you need to be accountable for the quality and success of the outcome of your work.

WHAT ARE YOU MOST PROUD OF IN YOUR CAREER?

My ability to touch co-workers in so many countries and cultures and hopefully leave the impression of being a fair boss, an inspiring leader and a great colleague. These are the things I treasure the most. When I came to Croatia after four years in China, my old team decided to come and visit me. Seven Chinese people travelled all that way just to say hello – I was bowled over that I meant something to the people, and that they felt they had developed under my leadership.

Working as an expat, you are often in a privileged situation. What makes me proud is when a local team steps up – when their eyes have a different light in them. That light was there, but was not always inspired and cultivated.

However, if you look at it from a CV point of view, what counts is what you generate for the business. In that regard, I'm proud of the work we did on the Tuborg brand – helping to take 'little brother' which had limited funding with no clear direction and mould the brand into what it is today – the biggest international brand in the Carlsberg group, the biggest in China, bigger than Carlsberg itself.

We created a community around it – of like-minded people, who thought in a nontraditional way. We didn't wear suits;

we came in like the youngsters, we played rock music. We were in Copenhagen, but supported the brand managers in all the markets. We encouraged people to be unconstrained in their thinking. We pushed the boundaries. Our motto was that it is easier to ask for forgiveness than for permission.

Recently, one of the guys in our executive team in Copenhagen, someone I had the pleasure of reporting to, introduced me to a group of people. He called me "the fairy godmother of Tuborg." My first reaction was, "OMG, this is so embarrassing," but later when I thought about it, I realized I couldn't get better praise or acknowledgement.

Then our EDP for Western Europe was giving a status update and said, "You all know Helle was the one who built the foundations of what makes Tuborg so big today." He gave me the recognition. I don't think women are programmed or used to this, but I must admit it did feel good to get some credit. We [women] don't cultivate it; we need somebody to give it to us.

DO WOMEN BRING ANYTHING UNIQUE TO MARKETING?

I believe we use our senses to a better degree than most men. We are more about 'feelings' than men. If I'm in a meeting, I might say, "This direction is good because I feel this is where the growth might be coming from." How often would you hear men say they are 'feeling' anything? An important part of marketing is that you have your senses open. You cannot create great marketing from just the numbers in the data, you have to go out there and sense it – go out into the supermarkets. In most countries, the shoppers for household goods are women, so intuitively we know what's going on in the shoppers' heads because we're doing it.

I have great respect for facts, but the way I use facts is different. Like lots of women, I use my intuition to get inspired, then I'll go back and question, "Do I have any facts that support that claim?" I see a lot of male colleagues who analyse the facts first, then go out to see the market. I think both ways are important – start from facts, start from intuition – both to run in parallel. We need both male and female marketers, we need personalities that complement each other, that work together.

Women are good at understanding people. They have insight into what is required to build teams. They are good at networking and they lead in a different way – it's less command and control, more inclusive – though there are differences between cultures, too.

YOU HAVE CONSIDERABLE INTERNATIONAL EXPERIENCE; WHAT'S YOUR PERSPECTIVE ON WOMEN IN MARKETING IN DIFFERENT PARTS OF THE WORLD?

From a global point of view, marketing is not a male-dominated industry. In the Western world, the US and Canada, are still male dominated, but it's not the case if you move outside of these areas. I worked a lot in developing overseas markets – Eastern Europe, Russia, Central Europe, Croatia, Serbia, Bulgaria – where 60–70% of all brand managers were women.

Currently the CMO, marketing director and VP levels are still more skewed towards males, but I'm encouraged that the talent pipelines indicate this is changing and becoming more female orientated. In some cultures, it is still extremely important for youngsters to go into a career that's acceptable for parents, and they often see things differently for their sons. It doesn't get as much face for the parents to say their son is a CMO, as it would be if he were a CFO. Interestingly, this can mean some men refrain from entering marketing, which makes marketing an excellent opportunity for women.

I HAVE ALWAYS BEEN
WILLING TO TAKE CHANCES.
I THINK THE REAL REASON
I BECAME A CEO WAS
BECAUSE I WAS CRAZY
ENOUGH TO ACCEPT IT.

– HELLE MULLER PETERSEN

WHAT NEEDS TO HAPPEN TO HELP BUILD EQUITY?

When I went to Croatia, the first piece of advertising I saw was an outdoor campaign for car batteries. It featured a porn model with a car battery between her tits. I was like, "F… – welcome back to western Europe." We need to understand this unconscious bias. And we need to be able to talk about these issues. At the moment, too many people ask, "What's your problem?" Or sigh, "Now she's talking about it again."

Journalists have a big responsibility. When Denmark had the first female premier, the media were obsessed with her Gucci bag. Have you ever seen them talking about a male premier's Hugo Boss suit?

As a woman, the bottom line is, if you marry a man who is not prepared to support your career, you will be pushing water uphill. I married a man who has been prepared to sacrifice part of his career – and he thought it was awesome.

The starting point is your life choices – you need to make choices and recognize that those choices will have implications. I could choose to stay home with my kids. We should recognize that women spending time with their kids learn skills too – women with kids are often better organizers.

Women are not good at taking credit for their work. When you first asked me to be interviewed, I initially said no. I was being modest; I didn't see myself as a Wonder Woman. I don't think this is unique – it's associated with a lot of females. We don't feel this need to go out into the public and take the glory, but we do get pissed off when some guy takes our credits. There are tons of women out there who have incredible stories we don't tell. We're not good at showing off, and perhaps it's time those stories were told by us or others.

PAT TAYLOR

Pat started in pharma sales as one of the first female reps for a small Swedish company that became part of Pharmacia, then Pfizer, where she was one of the first women to become a global brand marketing lead in big pharma.

During the interview, we talked about her journey from sales to marketing, the changes that took place in the pharma industry from being totally male dominated to a more diverse workforce, and her role in growing the Xalatan brand globally.

TELL US ABOUT THE START OF YOUR CAREER JOURNEY AS ONE OF THE FIRST WOMEN IN PHARMA.

I joined KabiVitrum in 1978, a small Swedish pharma company that had just started to employ female medical representatives. I entered a completely male-dominated industry, but it never bothered me. I just wanted to be successful and see where the journey took me.

In those days, the route into marketing in pharma usually started via sales because you had to learn all the scientific approaches in pharmaceutical selling, ABPI regulations, etc. Very few companies recruited marketers who didn't have pharma experience. Additionally, for the first decade of my career, all the marketers in KabiVitrum were male and the same was true of the other bigger pharma companies.

Working for a small progressive Swedish company that was more open minded meant I didn't feel locked out as a woman – I was lucky.

DID BEING A WOMAN CONTRIBUTE TO YOUR SUCCESS?

I never played the woman card. For me, it was always about who's best to get the job done.

I've seen many women use different techniques that exploit the fact they are a woman, but I was always completely against the flaunty, flirty side of gaining power. When I saw other reps with their short skirts and low-cut tops, I used to hate it. I wanted to be known as a really good rep, not the one with the biggest attributes!

However, there are a number of female characteristics that were an advantage. A woman's intuition to read and understand people and use all the signals to enable relevant communication. As a woman, you could strike a good professional relationship with a doctor. Relationship building was one of my strengths.

Additionally, I was good on the data and science and prided myself on my technical competence. The 'old school' male reps (who generally were not graduates) seemed less focused on all the scientific details, but for me that was another strength I could use to my advantage. You make your argument so robust that there's nothing anyone can catch you out on. I blended the scientific knowledge with building strong relationships – that combination led to my success.

One of the key success factors for a woman in a male-dominated world is to build respect for what you do, not for being female rather than male. My attitude was, if I've got to work extra hard to prove what I can do, then I'll do it. I'm not going to let being a woman get in the way, nor do I expect or want preferential treatment.

MY ATTITUDE WAS,
IF I'VE GOT TO WORK
EXTRA HARD TO PROVE
WHAT I CAN DO, THEN I'LL DO IT,
I'M NOT GOING TO LET BEING
A WOMAN GET IN THE WAY,
NOR DO I EXPECT OR
WANT PREFERENTIAL
TREATMENT.

– PAT TAYLOR

WHAT BARRIERS DID YOU FACE AS A WOMAN?

Resilience was important. It wasn't easy to get in to see a doctor with the receptionist as the interface, so you first had to win them over. Then there were some male doctors who wouldn't see female reps, so you had that to deal with that. You also had some doctors who thought they had the opportunity for the lingering handshake. I used to be very clear that that's not what I was there for. It was important to stand firm, deal with it and overcome those sorts of barriers.

I've never felt that being a woman has held me back because of the kind of mentality I have. I relish a challenge and the harder it is, the more I like it. Being told I couldn't do something would definitely spur me on.

What's interesting is that I never applied for a job, I just kept getting appointed and rose to a senior role that way. I wouldn't put myself up for something until I was 100% sure I could do it, so that may have affected my progress. Career progression for males was easier and their expectations higher.

TELL US ABOUT YOUR TRANSITION INTO A MARKETING ROLE.

I became a hospital rep, where I worked closely with and developed strong relationships with doctors on the wards, in theatre and intensive care units. Because I was so close to the 'customer' (the doctors), I brought the knowledge back to the marketing department, debriefed them and advised them on the campaign development.

I went into sales leadership and then into a training role, working across the whole company on scientific training as well as marketing. Because I was working with the reps on the marketing messaging, I became an extension of the marketing team; they would come to me to check out new campaigns. That's how I pivoted out of sales and into marketing.

Success in sales and training leadership led to my appointment as UK Business Unit leader for Ophthalmology and Oncology – the first woman to become a BU head in the UK – and in this role I had responsibility for both sales and marketing. My strength in sales, understanding of the customer and the science really stood me in good stead, and I began to understand how I could make a difference.

I also recognized that when working in pharma, and particularly rare diseases, the opinion leaders are fundamental to the business model, so I ran my own expert panels and global advisory boards with the top experts in the world. It became a big win for me. I was astounded at how customer-averse leadership teams could be.

I brought customer centricity into my business unit leadership. I ensured that my marketers spent time with customers. It became a core pillar of how we worked. Every member of the team had customer objectives that were measured and regularly reviewed.

WHAT ARE YOU MOST PROUD OF?

In 2003, I went to the US after Pharmacia was acquired by Pfizer. I became Global Brand Marketing Lead for Xalatan, an ophthalmic brand that is used to treat glaucoma. At that time, marketing was done in individual countries, so I had a fundamentally important remit to create a global brand and drive all the countries in the same direction with consistent core positioning and messaging.

I had previously been working with the multitude of European countries, so my strength was in the knowledge of the different markets and diversity within them. When I became global, I had to connect in all the other countries – the US, Japan, South America, etc. We did this by looking at the different countries and identifying common clusters, archetypes where similar approaches would work. We also created a global network of customers and opinion leaders we collaborated with regularly.

We took the brand from $400 million to $2 billion over its lifecycle, and I led it at the time of its most rapid growth. I'm immensely proud of that brand and the way we built it.

WHAT WAS YOUR APPROACH TO BUILDING SUCCESSFUL TEAMS?

I was fortunate to work with a woman who was an HR visionary. She opened up the archaic male-dominated organization to enable women to blossom and gain more of the senior leadership positions. She navigated her way so well that the men never felt threatened. She changed the shape of the organization and ran leadership programmes to help make them rounded in their approach. We didn't have any goals or quotas on how many women there should be in certain roles; it was her vision, commitment and influence on the senior leadership team that enabled roles to open up to women.

When you build an organization, the first thing to look at are the characteristics that the person brings to the team, rather than their gender. I always made sure my teams had a good mix of male and female, as I thought diversity was important to bringing different perspectives. But I never deliberately tried to make it 50/50 – it was about the best person for the job.

WHAT WERE YOUR GREATEST CHALLENGES?

In 2003, Pfizer acquired Pharmacia. Pfizer had a historical reputation for male dominance and arrogance, which resulted in the loss of much Pharmacia talent. Women in senior positions became less apparent; Pfizer was overpowering.

However, it started to change when a lady called Karen Katon became responsible for all the commercial marketing activities. Everyone was terrified of her, but in that environment and that point in time you probably needed a woman to be like that to pave the way.

I had been appointed to the role of Global Brand Marketing Lead on Xalatan because it had been a Pharmacia brand, and they wanted someone who had the necessary expertise and experience, but that meant I found myself back in a world where nearly all the other global leads were men.

It was a hard battle to fight, not just because I was a woman, but because I was from a smaller company. Pfizer thought no other company was as good as them – there was that kind of snobbery about being 'Pfizer born and bred.' But I did what I had always done – head down, work hard and build respect from within. I was able to achieve success within Pfizer, initially driving brand leadership, eventually becoming very integrated into the expanding organization and becoming Global Vice President for Multichannel Marketing.

Over time, Pfizer worked hard to build organizational diversity and change its ethos and culture.

It's an irony. As a young woman, I trailblazed in a male-dominated world by striving to be the best at what I did. In the latter days, I became frustrated that the politics, endemic within a company culture, were more complex and obstructive than male dominance had been.

I feel honoured to have had a hugely rewarding career in an amazing, rapidly changing pharmaceutical industry, worked with some truly inspirational leaders and high performing teams … just GREAT people!

SARAH HENWOOD

Sarah Henwood is CEO of the world's oldest practicing law firm, Thomson Snell & Passmore. She spent most of her career working in professional services, starting as the first graduate to be recruited into marketing at Price Waterhouse.

In the interview, we talked about her unplanned career path, her work attitude, having a great boss, EQ and why she's now happy to pour the tea and coffee.

WHY DID YOU CHOOSE MARKETING AS A CAREER INITIALLY?

I haven't had a completely planned career. At university, I did a summer internship at Price Waterhouse and was asked to come back and work in the marketing department. I studied psychology and had always been interested in marketing – understanding and influencing people's behaviour.

At PW I had a brilliant boss who said, "We have a grad programme for our accountants, so I'm going to construct a graduate programme for you in marketing." I had six months in database, six months in PR, six months in pitching, etc. I couldn't have asked for a better introduction into marketing at a professional level. It was very structured.

Then advertising came to the world of professional services. I had joined PW at a very exciting time. It was the first time accountants were allowed to advertise, and I was told I could work on the advertising campaign with Ogilvy and Mather. I landed on my feet!

After five years at PW, I ended up at YellowHammer advertising agency. Advertising in the 1980s was full-on.

The suits – those were the account execs – they would be hung out of the window if they failed to sell the creatives' ideas. It was a big culture shock after PW.

WHAT HAS LED TO YOUR SUCCESS?

I believe in working hard and well. In those days at PW, you weren't paid huge amounts, and I refused to be paid overtime because I was just doing my job. My boss recognized integrity, honesty and willingness for hard work. He had been an auditor and moved into the marketing world, so he wanted to make sure it was seen as a serious role.

Women work hard but are often modest about it and about their capabilities. They can be more reticent than men and question their own abilities and skill sets.

I recruit first and foremost on attitude. A lot of marketing is common sense. You can teach the technical skills, but attitude to learning, being curious and understanding what excellent client service looks like are paramount.

WHAT DO WOMEN UNIQUELY BRING TO MARKETING?

Men and women have different skill sets and different strengths, and you have to learn how to play those.

My boss at Ernst & Young was an audit partner. I remember one meeting I was very passionate about. I got upset emotionally and had to leave the room. After the meeting he called me in and said, "Never get embarrassed about showing your emotions, it shows your passions. We often see women crying as a weakness and men getting angry as a strength, but they're both expressing passions, each is valid."

I love learning. I have not had a vertical career – I've gone horizontally to acquire skills. I joined a change consultancy that specialized in using communication to effect change – my clients included Microsoft, who all sat in an open plan office but never talked to each other because their heads were in their computers. If you are going to change an organization, you have to change hearts as well as minds.

Emotional Intelligence is important. Marketing in the professional sector is about creating relationships – being able to ask questions, listen, hear and act. When you sit down and talk to clients, it's not me wanting to hear my voice, I just want to ask the questions and understand the answers. EQ has only relatively recently been valued and seen to represent a very important facet of why people buy. Women are assumed to have this naturally, but it's also a skill shared by many men.

Women are generally good at plate spinning and communication. Communication isn't what you say, it's what is received. I once did an NLP (neuro-linguistic programming) course and it was interesting to learn how people access the world in different ways and to acknowledge that in the way you communicate.

One of my bosses used to call me 'wiggly brain.' He'd bring me into meetings and say, "Just listen, I just want to hear what you think." I didn't come with set expectations or parameters.

Although I've had a couple of female bosses, the majority have been male. I've learned from men, so they must have these skills. They have seen these skills in me, and recognized and developed them.

One boss sent me on an assertiveness course. He said, "If you're going to hold your own in the environment of professional services, especially with lawyers who are used to arguing, you need to be more assertive." Some people were on the course because they were aggressive and needed to tone it down, some because they were mousey and needed to turn it up.

WHAT ARE YOU MOST PROUD OF IN YOUR CAREER?

I suffer from what a lot of others suffer – imposter syndrome. That aside, I'm proud of the fact that I've achieved lots of things. I've had the privilege of working with amazing organizations; the charity, The Outward Bound Trust; the Millennium Dome with Tony Blair when he was on his way to No 10; and I have travelled and lived in various places around the world and been several times to Buckingham Palace.

Personally, I'm most proud of being a single working mum, having an amazing son and continuing to have a successful career. It's bloody hard work. I had the most acrimonious divorce and still had to keep everything going.

WHAT HAVE BEEN THE CHALLENGES OF WORKING IN A MALE-DOMINATED ENVIRONMENT?

I've worked with some of the big law firms where it could be a rather macho culture, which was difficult to infiltrate. In such circumstances, women need encouragement to contribute.

It's not always men that are the problem. Some women climb the ladder and unfortunately turn into 'bitches.' I was once in a meeting with a female partner who sliced me down for no reason other than I was the only one in the room that she thought she could do that to. I spoke to her afterwards and asked her why she was doing it. I told her it was unhelpful, hurtful and demotivating. I was livid, but had to approach it in a mature, rational way and, hopefully, she learned from it.

I've worked with some great leaders – both men and women – and different situations require different types of leadership. Good leaders are the ones who have integrity and do the right thing even when no one is looking. They're also true to themselves and don't try to be something they're not. We all have strengths and weaknesses; it's understanding what they are and working within that.

TELL US ABOUT YOUR ROLE AS CEO IN THE WORLD'S OLDEST PRACTISING LAW FIRM.

I said no when I was first approached for this role because I was concerned about my work/life balance. Classic – if I can't do it 120%, I'm not going to put myself forward – typical woman. Then my son started secondary school, so I thought about it again and phoned the head-hunter.

One thing that counts for me is culture. I can be authentic here; I'm challenged and it's right for me. I have a long commute, but both the firm and I can be flexible and it's fine.

My partners have a great sense of humour. You have to have humour at work; you're a long time working.

The characteristics I value in my team, my partners and myself are around integrity and generosity. If you think of great people – men or women – they are people who are generous with their time, generous in experience, generous in making opportunities for you, generous in feedback.

I can be my authentic self now. It's difficult to do that when you're young. Admittedly, it's changing and the firm I now work for is all about bringing yourself to work. But back in the day, you had to play by the rules, had to put on your suit and your armour – don't be the person who goes and pours the tea and coffee. Now I'm very happy to pour the tea and coffee.

NEVER GET EMBARRASSED ABOUT SHOWING YOUR EMOTIONS, IT SHOWS YOUR PASSIONS. WE SEE WOMEN CRYING AS A WEAKNESS AND MEN ANGRY AS A STRENGTH, BUT THEY'RE BOTH EXPRESSING PASSIONS, EACH IS VALID.

– SARAH HENWOOD

ELAINE BARNES

Elaine is Chief Customer Officer at Cromwell Group Ltd. She started her career in sales and quickly realized it was all about understanding customer needs. She's passionate about the customer experience and sees it as integral to best-practice marketing.

During our interview, we discussed the advantage of working in a forward-thinking organization, being fearless, curious and continually learning, marrying the right partner, being customer led – not ego led –the importance of diversity and how ageism is as big an issue as sexism.

TELL US ABOUT THE STARTING POINT OF YOUR CAREER IN CUSTOMER EXPERIENCE AND MARKETING.
We should live our lives by design and not by default, but when I look back, my university degree had nothing to do with the job I ended up with. By default, I got into sales in an organization that, luckily, was very forward thinking for its time.

The Managing Director had a big impact and challenged me in amazing ways. This was the 1980s – an era when women were few and far between in leadership positions. He believed that women made better sellers and better leaders because we were fearless – we didn't know there were boundaries. I certainly did not. I went to an all-girls school and my parents told me I could be whatever I wanted.

He said, "I can't find anybody decent to do the job, so I'll give you the role." Those were his exact words! When I asked him what he meant, he said, "You don't look like a salesperson in my organization." At that time, a salesperson was tall, slim and blonde.

He was smart because he knew that would motivate me to prove him wrong. I thought, "Why should I not be successful because I didn't look or conform in a certain way?" I always had different-coloured hair – purple then bright red – it was all around kicking back at a stereotypical way of being. I focused on what I could do well and was incredibly successful there.

WHAT HAS LED TO YOUR SUCCESS IN GETTING TO A LEADERSHIP POSITION?

I have a natural curiosity, want to upset the status quo, and like to be pushed outside my comfort zone.

At Future, I was the only woman director. We were setting up the UK arm of an American electronics business. It was a marvellous experience setting up something from nothing and questioning, how are we going to make this a success? We were focused and worked incredibly hard. Our reputation and our ability to build relationships was key. That's when the customer experience piece came into play – it wasn't really talked about much in the 1980s. It was electronics and all very male-oriented. It was all about who could you go to the pub and football with. I didn't have that. I just had the ability to have conversations, to be interested, and to find out what's important to people.

I'm good at questioning and listening. It's not about you, it's about what you can give to other people. The value is about understanding and being curious.

When you're open and embrace learning, it's amazing what you can do. I'm working with some marvellous people today – data-driven, younger, and they think completely differently to me. Last year I did two RADA (Royal Academy of Dramatic Art) courses, which were phenomenal. One was around powerful presence and one was storytelling. It gives you validation and confidence that your story is worth telling. So many people are hidden because they don't feel that what they have to say is valuable.

People want to work for organizations that have a clear and strong understanding of their purpose. It's about seeing the difference you make by being customer led, not ego led. For example, rather than saying, "I'm going to do this because I'm important," saying, "We're doing this because our customers tell us this is important to them."

Look after your people - they are the ones who come first, because if your people are connected and enjoy what they're doing, you'll create a much better customer experience.

Business is getting much better at it. There's no such thing as five or ten-year plans any more. You've got to be agile, fluid and flexible. You have to have a longer-term vision that says what's my purpose, what are the values I'm going to live by, rather than having that big plan that says we're going to be a billion GBP company in ten years. Circumstances change and you have to be adaptable, curious and driven.

What also helped my success was that I was fortunate to be married to a partner who understood that my career was important to me. Make sure you marry somebody who doesn't have an ego and is prepared to understand and support you. We have two children and it's not always easy, but when you're in it together, that really helps.

WHAT'S THE BENEFIT OF MORE WOMEN IN BUSINESS AND MARKETING?

Women and diversity in the boardroom are critical. Matthew Syed's book, *Rebel Ideas*, is fascinating. It's about the need for diversity – if you always employ people like me, you will always think like me. It's a bit like when people say you've got great taste in music. What they mean is they like what you like.

Both women and men have the potential to have a range of characteristics. I've got some characteristics that might be more prevalent in a man – we're just people. Diversity of background, sexual orientation, gender can all make a difference.

I'm not into positive discrimination. I completely support not putting your sex or your age on an application form, but from then on, it's just about the right characteristics for the role.

Leadership today is very different. It isn't that triangle with me at the top, having to tell people what to do. It's about me being at the bottom of that triangle, supporting and challenging people to develop and grow. That's a real mindset shift – being a leader today is not about having all of the answers.

WHAT ARE THE THINGS YOU'RE MOST PROUD OF?

For me, it's just doing my job and seeing the impact I have on people. When I left Premier Farnell in North America, they presented me with a photograph album with a picture of Mary Poppins with my face on. Everybody had written something. When I left Future, I got a plaque that said thank-you for your courage, determination and friendship in growing Future from nothing to £500m.

IT'S INTERESTING YOU SAID THAT WAS JUST DOING YOUR JOB. IS THERE A TENDENCY FOR WOMEN TO JUST GET ON WITH THINGS WITHOUT PROACTIVELY SEEKING VALIDATION IN THE SAME WAY AS MEN?

If you were being stereotypical, you would say that men are much better at talking up what they do. They might have self-doubt about whether they can do a role, but they don't verbalize it. Men naturally see the things that they can do.

Even bold women tend to look at things and think – can I really do that? We have to support each other and say – go for it. Ask for help – it's OK to do that.

If marketing had been on the list of responsibilities required for my current role, I wouldn't have thought I could do the job. That's what women do – they have to tick all the boxes. Now it's become my responsibility, it's fine.

Women must have that complete surety, and it can hold them back.

WHAT ARE THE CHALLENGES YOU FACED AS A WOMAN?

Guilt is a barrier and a challenge. When I went to Farnell and had these amazing opportunities to go around the world and transform a business, my kids were in their early teens. Although my husband was really supportive, I felt guilty. I don't know whether men feel the guilt – they probably do, but society says they don't have to. They compartmentalize it better.

The other challenge is that if I'm given a role, then I feel 120% responsible, even though I'm part of a team. The barrier I must overcome is me. When I feel I'm not good enough, not doing what needs to be done quickly enough, I can't think straight, and then I tend to think, well I'm obviously not right for this. Then I take a step back and write down all the reasons why I CAN do it.

I've never been in a situation where I haven't been given an opportunity because I'm a woman. What's really interesting, though – when you start a new role in a new company in a senior position at 57 – and somebody said to me, "It's really unusual; most people your age would be thinking about retiring."

It was a joke. However, would the same have been said to a man?

I DON'T KNOW WHETHER MEN FEEL THE GUILT – THEY PROBABLY DO, BUT SOCIETY SAYS THEY DON'T HAVE TO.

– ELAINE BARNES

CATHERINE QUERNÉ

Catherine is Strategy Director at Brittany Ferries. She joined the company after business school and has remained inspired by the ethical vision of its founder ever since. It was while working in duty-free that she got her education in marketing, learning from the iconic perfume brands and whisky houses.

During our interview, we talked about coming from a humble background, her love of learning and what it's like to be a woman among sailors!

TELL US ABOUT YOUR CAREER PROGRESSION AND HOW YOU GOT INTO MARKETING.

My parents were modest farmers in Brittany. At school I was good in maths and science, so at 14 I went to boarding school (*en pensionnat*), where I passed the scientific *baccalaureate*.

From there, I went to business school in Angres for four years. I did internships in the third and fourth years, spending six months working at Brittany Ferries, six months at business school. I also did a diploma in chartered accountancy.

My first role at Brittany Ferries was with on-board services as a revenue controller, where I identified missing profit opportunities. Then I moved to be a buyer of all the on-board products – meat, cutlery, toilet paper, everything – but still with responsibility for profit and revenue.

In the 1990s, I did a range of courses at Instead International Business School. That is where I learned that you can't ask the world to change but you can instigate change yourself. I also learned how to observe, how to make things happen, what to consider before you make a decision. Business school gives you food for thought, time to reflect, you meet executives from all over the world with broad experience and you learn to see things differently.

In 1996, Brittany Ferries nearly went bankrupt. We had to look closer at the margins and the best were in the duty-free business. I said to my boss, "That's where we must push." And that's how I got into marketing.

IT WAS TAKING ON THE DUTY-FREE BUSINESS THAT LED YOU TO MARKETING?

The duty-free market is rich and interesting in terms of marketing because it means working internationally with perfume houses, whisky groups, deluxe brands and tobacco companies. I worked with Nina Ricci, Guerlain, Yves St Laurent, Chanel and learned a lot about branding; how some of the brands were losing their soul, how they needed to stick to their vision. I also worked with big organizations such as United Distillers, which is now Diageo. Every year they organized a conference for the buyers with all the latest thinking in marketing, shopper behaviour and technology.

That was an interesting time of learning. I love discovering new ways. I love new ideas and like to challenge my own beliefs.

The year 2000 was the end of duty-free, so we had to reinvent ourselves. I was in charge of the move to classic sales without the advantage of lower prices. We had to create services so people would continue to shop on-board, so we created stories.

Then I was promoted to On-board Services Director. For the first four years, I was co-director with a guy who was quite different from me, but we shared the same human and ethical values. We were successful because we had complementary skills and trusted each other. He had good intuition and my maths skills enabled me to do the calculations and analysis to back up his intuitive thinking.

WHAT WERE THE CHALLENGES YOU FACED AND HOW DID YOU OVERCOME THEM?

In 2016, I was off for six months with burnout. I was exhausted! I was fortunate to stop early enough before it got bad, and I had the caring support of good friends. I was too perfectionistic, naïve and oversensitive.

The maritime transport world is traditional male-orientated. Male energy is more about a cause equalling a result; it must be factual, measurable, tangible and direct. Conversely, feminine energy is not always measurable; it is more indirect, ineffable, on another level of logic. Each human being has these two energies, and I believe that organizations need to heed this female part in their management strategy. I am proud to say that Brittany Ferries is moving fast in that direction.

It was difficult to come back to work as 'burnout' means you failed and are weak. I didn't get my director job back. I had to be very resilient and dig in to explore my core values, analyse my behaviours, seek my resources. Then I found the key for wellbeing at work: confidence resides inside us, not outside. Confidence leads to better analysis and performance.

I was asked to work on the brand positioning project. I enjoyed working alongside brand consultants and the digital transformation team, and they gave me positive feedback on collaboration, which resulted in me working on more strategic projects.

I also learned I can trust my intuition. When you act in a man's world (industrial), you can lose your senses (instinct) or trust them less because you are regularly asked to demonstrate them rationally. Now I say, "Take it or leave it. If you feel it is interesting, then we can explore it." You probably need to be more senior to do that!

I am interested in neuroscience. It is similar to the Buddhist vision on the nature of reality and the way people act and why. I learned about how the brain works and human psychology. It strengthened my trust in people, gave me new ways of thinking and sharing, and insights to be less judgmental. I believe each person has their own wisdom and with trust and good listening, efficient solutions are found. It changed the way I see the world; I don't restrict the universe to my own views.

WHAT ARE THE UNIQUE CHARACTERISTICS THAT WOMEN BRING TO MARKETING AND LEADERSHIP?

Marketing is quite a feminine world – it's easier to share your views and get your points understood.

Leadership is not so straightforward. Being in the masculine maritime world, I had to work hard to convince others. You need to prove you are right to gain trust. When you are knowledgeable and know what you're talking about, you earn their respect and your ideas are taken on. We need male and female voices in a collaborative environment of respect and trust where ideas can be listened to.

WHAT ARE THE CHALLENGES AS A WOMAN IN MARKETING AND BUSINESS?

Women need to prove more, which takes a lot of time and energy. Women try to do things as men do, but they are not men, they are women. It's less of an issue now, but I used to feel the need to comply with the majority who were men – I felt I should act the same way. It was my mistake!

Most women are naturally not as good at competing – it's not about winning or losing for them. The guys often don't listen fully; instead, they're evaluating what it means for them. They look at you as if you're mad with your out-of-the-box ideas. Then a few months later, someone declares, "I have a good idea and it's important and urgent." It's the idea you were trying to express based on your intuition. We must accept, though, that women could be pushier with their communication!

I do think women's voices should be heard. A good balance of men and women would provide a livelier, more productive and more inclusive work environment. It is important to listen and learn from different points of view. When we work together, we are bigger.

Within the company now, there's more openness and respect for different perspectives. On the board, nearly 40% are women and when a woman talks, she's listened to. The guys don't always follow, but then we don't always follow them either!

WHAT DO YOU THINK THE FUTURE HOLDS?

I'm now working on bringing the brand positioning to life in the business, which includes the art and interior design on the new ships. I'm in charge of creating the story and choosing the creatives. I feel an internal energy, would like to be more creative myself and express myself artistically. Perhaps it was a little hidden and I've set it free!

People are often lost in their brain and mind – we should have more confidence in our senses. We've been in a very intellectual period. It has been masculine and data driven. The future is more about feelings, sensory, spiritual.

I may be a dreamer, but I believe people will choose companies where their work and actions will contribute to a more humane, supportive and united society.

WE'VE BEEN IN A VERY INTELLECTUAL PERIOD. IT HAS BEEN MASCULINE, AND DATA DRIVEN. THE FUTURE IS MORE ABOUT FEELINGS, SENSORY, SPIRITUAL.

– CATHERINE QUERNÉ

1990s–2000s
GIRL POWER

These Wonder Women entered their careers in the 1990s –2000s amid the third wave of feminism. The third wave argued that the second wave overemphasised experiences of upper middle-class white women, rather than seeing women's lives as intersectional; demonstrating how race, ethnicity, class, religion, and nationality are all significant factors. It embraced individualism and diversity.

It was characterized by many causes, including a critique of the portrayal of women in the media, as well as campaigns against rape culture and sexual harassment. Punk rock riot grrrls were hitting the scene, demanding to be heard and, in academia, women's studies was shifting from feminist theory focused solely on women to considering gender more broadly.

In careers, women had greater ability to 'shatter the glass ceiling,' seek out opportunities for leadership, to explore, experiment, and focus on their own personal and career development. Many more women have reached higher levels in corporations, law firms and government.

GEMMA GREAVES

As founder of Cabal, co-founder of Nurture and the former chief executive of The Marketing Society, Gemma loves bringing people together by creating events and unique experiences where you get to be you. She believes that if interesting and interested people come together, magic happens and the biggest impact is made.

During the interview, we talked about how building relationships and collaboration leads to success, don't be afraid to make big asks, and how being asked to step up to the chief exec role at the Marketing Society when she was on maternity leave led to her being brave.

HOW DID YOU GET INTO A CAREER IN MARKETING?

Initially I hadn't considered marketing because I wanted to be a TV presenter. At university, I did a student placement at The Foreign and Commonwealth Office. They made incredible documentaries about the relationship between Britain and foreign countries. My time there became a defining moment in my career because it helped me identify my strengths as well as what I did and did not want to do.

Although I was employed as an office administrator, I found that the more I showed interest, curiosity and was helpful, the more opportunities outside my original role arose. I made myself really useful to the producers and, in turn, learned all about the documentaries we were making.

I noticed we were spending a huge amount of money on copyright clearance and realized there might be an opportunity to do it a different way. When I spoke to the producer in charge, she was very excited and supportive, but when I took the idea to the more junior associate producer, she laughed in my face and said, "No, this is the way it works. But, if you think you can do better, then be my guest." After picking myself up off the floor, I decided to have the courage of my convictions. Within a few days, I made a significant commercial impact, and I was fortunate enough to take the lead role on that project and others.

When I talk to people starting out, I always ask them what they want to achieve. I tell them to think about how they can stand out and make an impression, and that they shouldn't be afraid to make big asks. I believe too many of us stay silent and, as a result, don't progress in the way we could. We all need to encourage and nurture others.

The early experiences at a number of different organizations I worked for made me realize how much I loved creating partnerships and mutually beneficial wins. For me, it's about people: building relationships – understanding what makes people tick, how to get under their skin, creating collaborations that are successful on all sides. This has been the constant in my career and has helped define my success.

When I joined The Marketing Society, I knew I had found my home. I realized it was time to inject new energy, build something memorable and that I'd only achieve this by surrounding myself with an amazing team whose strengths complemented my own. That's when my journey properly began.

WHAT ARE YOU MOST PROUD OF?

Three things. First, becoming chief executive of the Marketing Society at the age of 37, where I launched the 'Brave' agenda and spearheaded the Society's global expansion.

I wasn't the typical profile for chief exec of an association like The Marketing Society, given my age and my gender. My boss, Hugh Burkitt, met me for lunch when I was on maternity leave and my son, Joshie, was only two months old. I remember it vividly. I went to a monkey music class with Joshie in the morning, then I had lunch with Hugh, expecting it to be the normal catch up, but he said, "I think the time is right for you to step up and for me to step back."

Hugh was an amazing mentor, role model and has been a big part of my career. There was no doubt in my mind that I was ready to step up to lead the organization, but the question I asked myself was whether I needed to "be more Hugh" or "be more me." I quickly realized I just needed to be myself.

That was the start of the 'Brave' agenda. I realized that in a very vulnerable and public space, the only way I could succeed was to be my true self, especially if I wanted to encourage others to be brave. That started the whole journey of discovery, which has turned into a global conversation and is embedded into our purpose and everything we do. The insight I learned is it's when you are your true, authentic self that you will be your best self.

So, now we talk about us as humans, not just marketers, we explore subjects that matter to us all such as mental health, confidence, wellbeing, leadership, gender, race and diversity. We're tackling taboos, pushing boundaries, creating comfortable spaces to have the uncomfortable conversations that need to happen. That's how I believe together we can make change.

The second thing I am most proud of is becoming an entrepreneur and creating Cabal. It's a boutique club of hand-picked, incredible people, based on the ethos that if you bring good people together, good stuff happens. It's been my side hustle until now, but it will soon become my main focus along with Nurture, which is in its beta phase.

I launched Cabal in 2013 while working at The Marketing Society and could do this because I was given flexibility and trust. Flexibility has been an important part of my career, for any teams and businesses I have led. For me, it's not about how much time you spend on something, it's about output – what you deliver and what you achieve.

Third, and personally, I'm most proud of being a mum to Joshie. I honestly feel that becoming a parent has made me a better leader. I'm constantly learning from Joshie – empathy, listening, resilience, patience, negotiation. My son negotiates with me all the time and often wins!

WHAT BENEFITS DO WOMEN BRING TO MARKETING?

Marketing plays to the stereotypical female strengths of empathy, understanding people and building relationships, but I know lots of great male leaders who have these strengths too. It's not about gender; it's about the person.

Women get each other as women. When you haven't got men in the room, the conversation is deeper, more honest, more exposing. The more you can create those safe spaces where people can be themselves – for both women and men – then you can create an advantage. As a marketer, it's about breaking down those barriers and seeing people as themselves and truly understanding the customer.

There are Wonder Women and Supermen all around us – it's about us as a community encouraging, helping and supporting each other to rise. I see incredible people who may be more introverted, less into shouting about their achievements, but we're not seeing them. We have a responsibility as role models and mentors to create spaces where everyone gets to shine.

DON'T BE AFRAID TO MAKE THE BIG ASKS.

– GEMMA GREAVES

WHAT HOLDS PEOPLE BACK?

Modesty and fear of ridicule. As we get older and wiser, we need to be proud of what we've achieved, become role models and encourage others to achieve great things too. It's not self-congratulatory – it helps others to learn, grow and be inspired.

Self-limiting beliefs hold us back; those voices in our head that tell us we are not good enough, smart enough. I have recently been doing talks on imposter syndrome and my only qualification is that I have it (deeply) – it's a fear of being found out and the feeling that what we have achieved is merely through luck as opposed to our abilities. Over 70% of people have it, but we rarely talk about it. In fact, calling it a syndrome is misleading; it is universal but rarely talked about. The way we can begin to overcome it is first to acknowledge it, talk about it, then to feel the fear and do it anyway.

WHAT ARE THE CHALLENGES FOR A WOMAN IN MARKETING?

In everything I've done, I haven't thought about myself through the lens of being a woman in business; instead, I have always been motivated and ambitious to achieve my top potential. Having said that, becoming a parent can present huge challenges, depending on the company culture and support system. Marketing is so fast paced, whether agency or client-side, that it's not easy to juggle family and work and hold down a career. That's why flexible working is so important for all parents, not just women. Everything in my life is based around nursery drop-off and pick-up, and because of that I've become more efficient. As a parent, you have to make choices, prioritize, at times compromise, and do what is right for you and your family.

Women generally take the career break, though, and with this comes challenges around confidence. If you're out of work for a while, you can start to doubt yourself. Skill sets change. Marketers now need to wear so many hats and move at a quick pace. We need more support systems to help women back to work.

We need to share all the positive stories about women's achievements, celebrate each other's successes, and help others who need it.

WHAT ADVICE WOULD YOU LEAVE US WITH?

Ultimately, I believe men and women together are stronger, together we will achieve great things and together we can make change happen.

So:

1. Be you, so others can be them.
2. Be kind; everyone you meet is facing a great battle.
3. Stand out; make an impression and find your way to have an impact.

KARA MCCARTNEY

Kara has an impressive list of top agencies and clients on her CV. She started her career as a social analyst at Ammirati Puris Lintas, found her passion for brand strategy at Landor, and is now senior vice president of The Value Engineers in San Francisco.

During our interview, we talked about how marketing is in her blood, how she thrives when working with corporations that have a problem and need a brand renovation, and how proud she was to change one company's attitude to working mothers.

HOW DID YOU GET INTO A CAREER IN MARKETING?

My parents were both in the fashion industry and were business-minded people, so our dinner conversations as I was growing up were about brand and marketing, especially in the exciting world of fashion. That was my life – it was in my blood!

I also had a cousin who was very successful in advertising. I interned for her agency when I was 18 and the experience had a big impact on me. It was a boutique agency in New York called Ammirati & Puris, and they had created some legendary campaigns, such as The Ultimate Driving Machine for BMW, and The Tightest Ship in the Shipping Business for UPS. I found my niche. It was the blend of creativity, ideas and discovery that drew me in.

I worked with some remarkable people there, but the one person who had a big influence on what I wanted to do in marketing was Alan Causey, who pioneered a lot of generational marketing. His focus was on understanding the social shifts and helping companies anticipate what's coming, forcing them to look beyond their product and their industry and into the world of their customers and society as a whole. Alan had tremendous presence, but it was his curiosity that really made him sparkle.

When I finished college, I did a few different things, largely in fashion, but went back into advertising when Alan Causey created his own department focused on Social Analysis and Forecasting, at the now global Ammirati Puris Lintas. We did a lot of work for Unilever in those days, demonstrating how the world was changing around them from gender roles to attitudes toward cultural difference. Take detergent, for example. Our focus was not just on the detergent product or the target customer; we were thinking about how laundry fits into the broader scheme of what's going on in the world. We looked at it from a bigger perspective and that hadn't been done before.

My personal curious spirit was cultivated at Sarah Lawrence College, a leading liberal arts college in New York, which was known for its pioneering approach to education. Its ethos was around thinking beyond the brief, even for your own independent scholarly studies; it was about designing your own academic future and developing intellectual curiosity.

So, that was who I was. Looking beyond a single product was where my passion lay.

BEWARE OF STEREOTYPES AND ASSUMPTIONS!

– KARA MCCARTNEY

WHAT WERE THE DEFINING MOMENTS IN YOUR CAREER THAT HELPED YOU SUCCEED?

My career really took off when I moved to Landor in San Francisco and into brand strategy and design. I love thinking about things in a creative way, trying to isolate what the real challenge is within a business culture and how can we help design programmes to unlock the potential of that organization. A lot of what we did was corporate marketing. When a business had gone through an awkward merger or was starting to tank after years of being a strong brand, they would come to Landor and need a rebrand. That's an exciting place to be. But you're also dealing with corporations that are often stuck in their ways. They may think they just need a new logo or look and feel system, but what they really need is a culture shift.

That's where I started to really thrive. It was taking the skills of being an ethnographer, the skills of someone who loves consumers and generational marketing and applying it to corporations.

WHAT ARE YOU MOST PROUD OF IN YOUR CAREER?

This is going to sound crazy, but I am most proud of changing the way that one of the companies I worked for thought about working mothers. It was a pretty radical change. There were women in powerful positions on the executive team, but none of them had children. All the senior men had stay-at-home wives. Historically, any woman at the company who got pregnant left.

The assumption was that I would leave because I was pregnant – everyone just laughed about it. During my pregnancy, I was on bed rest for two months and I worked the whole time. I even joked with my MD that he should hire more women on bed rest because they have nothing better to do than work 24/7. I was always very vocal and visible, happy to share what I was thinking and doing. Then my daughter was born two months early and had to be in the NICU (neonatal intensive care unit). I wasn't allowed to stay at the hospital, so a week after giving birth, I went back to work. I needed to do something – I couldn't just sit at home. I worked for a month before I could bring my daughter home.

It paid off because I was able to prove time and time again that I would live up to what was expected of me in my job. I would go above and beyond, and people recognized that I was not working less because I was a mother.

Attitudes and behaviour in the organization changed, and that made a difference for other women too. Women who thought they were being supportive by making decisions on my behalf as a mother, for example, about late-night calls with clients, realized that was worse than me making that choice myself. Having that dialogue was something that the organization had never done before.

WHAT HAS BEEN YOUR EXPERIENCE AS A WOMAN IN MARKETING?

Even today, I experience surprising behaviour. This is a recent example. I asked a male client a question, then he pivoted his body to respond to the 25-year-old male in my team. I don't minimize the fact that certain individuals feel more comfortable with talking to men – they are less comfortable talking to women – and you want people to feel comfortable, relaxed and to share things. My dad was a WWII marine, a tough guy with a heart of gold. He really raised me more like a son, so I've always felt very comfortable around guys. That makes it all the stranger when I experience men behaving in that way.

Interestingly, in New York, many of the ad agencies I worked with were run by women, and women were important people, so I didn't feel a lot of gender bias. When I moved to Publicis Hal Riney in San Francisco 20 years ago one of our clients was Saturn, so there were a lot of men focused on the automobile market. Without a doubt, there was a sense that women were 'those pretty things.' It was shocking to me.

We don't have a problem with the younger generation of men. They are much more attuned and respectful of women. More and more male parents are talking about childcare issues – it's wonderful that it's become part of the conversation. Thirty years ago, you would never talk about your children or family at work, you would hide that you are a mom, but now it's how you bond.

ARE THERE FEMALE CHARACTERISTICS THAT MAKE WOMEN GOOD AT MARKETING?

Everyone talks about women multitasking, focussing on detail, focussing on others versus oneself, but we have to be careful of the stereotypes. I don't believe there really is a difference, especially when you look at the younger generation.

We need to pay attention to our audiences. As women, we cannot assume that we understand what women (and men) need and want. We need to uncover what they need and want. Looking at our employees, our clients, how we talk to consumers – once we start making assumptions, we're minimizing the potential.

So, beware of stereotypes and assumptions!

WHAT ARE THE CHALLENGES AS A WOMAN
IN MARKETING?

There have been a million small things – a million small gestures that I can't even remember. That's what makes it difficult to fight against.

As a freelance ethnographer, I worked on a project for a detergent brand, travelling all over the country talking to moms in their peer groups in homes. One of the most powerful things I realized is that, as mothers, women care about their children and their families, but it's so easy to lose their sense-of-self – and that is the one similarity that all of them had. I would hazard a guess that, as young men become more and more a part of the process of parenting, the more likely it is for them to have that same sensation. It's an interesting phenomenon as a marketer.

KATE THORNTON

Kate spent over 20 years of her career at British Airways in a variety of sales, commercial, marketing and customer roles, both overseas and in the UK. More recently, she was chief customer officer at Simplyhealth.

During our interview, we discussed how she came up with a groundbreaking idea for a campaign at BA, how if you ask you might just get, why imposter syndrome is a strength, the power of pursuing the things you are passionate about, how the conversation should be around diversity and inclusion, not just gender, and why you should wear fuchsia pink.

DID YOU SPECIFICALLY CHOOSE A CAREER IN MARKETING?

I actually started in a customer service role with British Airways in Scandinavia. I loved dealing with customers. I then went into a commercial role and was asked to put together a pricing campaign to drive volume. My boss loved the idea and very generously said, "You came up with the campaign idea, so you can talk to the agency and help design the creative." I ran the first two-for-one campaign they had ever seen. People were queueing down the stairs in all four Nordic capitals, so that was big news in British Airways.

Looking back, it was a laughably simple campaign, but everybody was scratching their heads on how to generate volume. It became a global campaign – two for one in 70 destinations worldwide run across multiple European markets. At the time it was groundbreaking.

I got asked to talk about it at the European Marketing meeting, which was at the Ritz Carlton in Barcelona. I thought, this is the job to be in – I can get to hang out in swanky hotels! That's not the most career-focused answer.

HAVE THERE BEEN OTHER DEFINING MOMENTS IN YOUR CAREER?

Until recently, I would have said my career was shaped by luck, but actually I worked hard, and people helped me. Men predominantly helped me, as they were the ones in the senior roles. I also now realize that it has more to do with my characteristics, the requests and decisions I made and how I made the most of opportunities.

Recently, I spoke at a local secondary school for International Women's Day about three lessons I have learned: 1) if you ask, you might just get, 2) sometimes, things that can be perceived as weaknesses can be strengths, 3) the power of pursuing things you are passionate about.

There were two big points when my career took off based on the principle of *'If you ask, you might just get.'* The first was when I was 28 and put up my hand to become sales and marketing manager in Norway. I was running all the BA commercial activity – very much the public face of BA. It happened because I put my hand up.

The second happened when I was working for Kerris Bright (then BA marketing director) in London and she announced she was leaving and BA was looking externally for candidates. For many years, I would just have sat back and swallowed that, but I made a conscious decision to see Kerris and ask for help. Was BA going externally, telling me I don't have the potential to step up into a head of marketing role? Or were there development gaps that nobody had talked to me about? In which case, what are they?

Kerris is inspirational – she gave me a lot of confidence. She helped with an approach to apply for the job and that triggered a sequence of events that enabled me to demonstrate what I was made of in terms of leadership. I ended up in a different role, running the product and service agenda at BA, but ultimately a more exciting role for me as it was all about the customer experience, and the British Airways brand IS the customer experience. Of course, it's also the advertising and communications, but for customers, it's about what they're seeing, feeling and experiencing. That was a decisive point in my career because I decided to go and ask for it.

I've seen research and talked to other women about it. Women, on average, will look to match 80% to 90% of the criteria on a job profile before applying, while men stop at about 30%.

It's very complex. There's always a danger that women feel they are not getting opportunities because men aren't giving them the opportunities.

How is anyone supposed to know what my ambition is if I'm never going to tell them?

WHY DO YOU THINK WOMEN ARE MORE HESITANT ABOUT PUSHING THEMSELVES FORWARD?

Sometimes women are judged differently. My generation was brought up with different expectations. I remember in the 1970s watching the Blue Peter team burying the box for the year 2000. I said to my mother, "When they dig that up, I will be 31 and I will be sitting on a sofa with my children watching them do it." That's what I assumed I would be doing! There's no way my brothers assumed that.

Within my family, I was the first woman in my generation to aspire to a professional career. I recently went to my 30-year college reunion at Cambridge and was flabbergasted to be reminded that I was in only the ninth or tenth year of women in-take.

WHAT CHARACTERISTICS DO WOMEN UNIQUELY BRING TO MARKETING AND LEADERSHIP?

There are some stereotypical answers. It's never that clear cut that women have 100% of these qualities and 100% of men have others.

Imposter syndrome can be a strength – it means women are more curious, we listen and are more open-minded. If you are super confident that you are right the entire time, that limits your ability to consider other perspectives. Great breakthroughs come from listening, considering the facts, being prepared to take a slightly different angle, to do something fresh.

Arguably, men take more risks. There is also more tolerance of men making mistakes, but maybe they're just better at how they present them. If you start in a position of self-doubt, there's a danger you present mistakes as mistakes rather than bold bets that didn't quite come off.

One advantage of being a woman is it's easier to stand out. At BA leadership forums, 75% of the senior managers would be men in grey suits. I made it a rule to turn up in fuchsia pink!

As more women come into marketing and business, it's up to women to organize themselves into networks to counterbalance the male networks, but without creating a dissonance. Women also need to become the bosses who help push other women forward. It's easier when there are people who help you – whether they are senior people who can mentor or champion you or peers that you can just bounce things off.

I THINK THE CONVERSATION SHOULD BE AROUND DIVERSITY AND INCLUSION, NOT JUST GENDER. ENCOURAGE PEOPLE TO SEE DIVERSE VIEWPOINTS, STYLES, AND CHARACTERISTICS.

– KATE THORNTON

HAVE YOU FACED ANY CHALLENGES OR DIFFICULT SITUATIONS BECAUSE YOU'RE A WOMAN?

On an explicit level, not so much.

It's much harder to quantify the stuff that's going on below the surface. When you come up through an organization where the majority of senior leaders are men – what's the impact of that network, that conversation and the way they socialize, on your ability to be seen as part of it?

Women have brilliant ideas, but how many times have we been in meetings and said something that was ignored, then a man says the same thing. Everyone says, "Well done, Geoff, that was very clever." Men can be better at presenting their ideas with confidence and cutting through.

I think the conversation should be around diversity and inclusion, not just gender. Encourage people to see diverse viewpoints, styles and characteristics.

I have met monstrous women. Equally, I recruit amazing men into my teams.

There are big marketing names who are men, but I probably know more female marketers than I do male. It doesn't feel particularly male dominated. Marketing feels more balanced.

KATHY LEECH

Kathy is executive director of corporate brand and advertising for the technology and media innovator, Comcast. She's highly experienced in crisis management, having led BP's US advertising and social media response during the 2010 Gulf oil spill, which ultimately helped BP improve trust and favourability metrics and earned BP the number-three rank among social media programs at FTSE companies.

During our interview, we talked about learning from a crisis, how to cope with being called "sugar" and "honey," how to deal with conflict in a controlled fashion, why you should trust your intuition but get the data to back up your story.

WAS YOUR CAREER IN MARKETING PLANNED?
I always joke that I'm a recovering accountant. When I studied accountancy at university, Texas was going through an oil slump and accountancy was the only way to get a job. I also thought it would be a sound business foundation for any career.

I worked at Quaker in accounting for the marketing team and enjoyed how passionate, fun and stimulated they were and thought, this is something I want to do. So, I got my MBA and joined the marketing team.

I've worked in marketing for Quaker, Amoco, BP and now Comcast. What I love most is the combination of insights into action.

WHAT WERE THE HIGHS AND LOWS OF YOUR CAREER?

The best and the worst was the Gulf oil spill. The good was it was like getting a PhD in crisis management – long and intense days working with PR teams, legal and operations. We had to respond to the crisis, then rehabilitate the brand. It was a unique experience.

It was tough at the time, as I had a ten-month-old and we were away at the Houston crisis centre for 10 to 12 days at a time. Even when we were back home, it was still 24/7. But there was a real sense of satisfaction that we were able to help the community that was impacted. Brand favourability had fallen 20 points, so once the crisis was over, we had to rebuild the brand over the next five years.

WHAT CHALLENGES DID YOU FACE AS A WOMAN IN MARKETING?

Quaker was really open to women in marketing, but it was different at Amoco. They had gone through a McKinsey audit and decided to revamp their entire marketing team, which had previously been all men. The men were reassigned or laid off and replaced by 20- to 30-year-old women. The owners of the retail gas stations we worked closely with were not pleased, and I remember one challenging incident when someone was ranting about how unfair the change was. He was angry with me even though the decision to change the marketing organization happened long before I joined. Frustrated, I finally said to him, "Have I offended you? Have I done something wrong?" He said no, and from then on, we worked together positively.

I worked closely with the people who owned the retail gas stations. Most of them were white males in their 50s and 60s, so often I was the only woman in a meeting of 10 to 15 people. I had to figure out how to get their agreement on the marketing programmes we wanted them to implement on their sites. I'm 5'1" and blonde, so I decided to play into the fact that I was their daughters' age. I didn't push back at being called "sugar" or "honey" – I just related to them as people and tried to get to know them. For me, sometimes a stealth approach is better than directly confronting sexism. Ultimately, I won them over, and we worked closely together. They ended up funding the Amoco racing programme, which was a big win.

My husband calls me the velvet hammer!

Some of the worst experiences I've had were working for insecure female bosses. With a male boss who's insecure, you can support him and make sure he looks good. They don't see you as a threat and usually the relationship works out. When a female boss is insecure, there's an element of rivalry and that's very difficult.

WHAT ARE YOU MOST PROUD OF IN YOUR CAREER?

Being a mother of two boys who are happy and healthy and managing a career is the first thing!

On a purely professional level, at BP and at Comcast, I led branding programmes that made a difference. The 'aha' moment for BP was to understand through a PATH analysis what was the relevant messaging two years after the spill. It showed that until we spoke about safety, no one cared about innovation or community service. So, we spoke about safety and over the next five years, favourability improved, and we were then able to move to other messages.

I did the same thing here at Comcast and found that customer service was key. Figuring out relevant messaging, in what order and aligning the company behind it is the important thing.

BEING A MOTHER MAKES ME A BETTER LEADER AND MARKETER.

– KATHY LEECH

WHAT IMPACT DOES BEING A MOTHER HAVE ON A WOMAN'S CAREER IN MARKETING?

Being a mother makes me a better leader and marketer. My son plays video games and is online all the time. Just by listening to him, I can figure out some of the things that are coming. For example, he was on Twitch, so I knew that was a channel to watch from an advertising perspective. The fact that he doesn't watch TV told me four years ago that it's not part of the mix if we want to reach younger people.

We have a two-career family. My husband was an attorney, he's now a mediator and the fact that he was unable to move has had an impact on my career. But I wouldn't change it because together the relationship is strong, and the children have had both of us present.

Would it have been better for my career if my husband had been nonworking? Absolutely. I see that with a lot of strong women in the organization who have the support of a husband in the same way that some nonworking wives support their husbands. But I will take slightly less career advancement for a more centred and 360-degree life.

In the US, most women come back into the workforce three or four months after having a baby. There's an acceptance here that you can be both a good employee and a good mom.

Having children does make you slow down, be aware of nuances and be more tuned into people. One of my skills is reading people, which is even better now I'm a mom.

WHAT SKILLS DO WOMEN HAVE THAT MAKE THEM GOOD AT MARKETING?

The good marketers have an intuitive understanding of their customer and target audience, and women tend to be more comfortable with their emotional side. My husband did some legal focus groups and he described how he took notes of everything everyone said and counted it all up to understand the key themes, whereas his female colleague just sat back and listened and at the end was able to summarize everything. There's no right or wrong – just different approaches.

Intuition is good, but you need the data to support your story. Sometimes your emotions will lead you astray. When we do research, I sit down with my team and say, I think the story is going to be this, but let's see if the numbers hold that up. Sometimes I'm wrong and that's fine. That means we're learning something new.

WHAT HOLDS WOMEN BACK?

Women are often too modest and too ready to say sorry. I apologized to our CMO (who's male) for having the wrong presentation deck and he said to me, "Kathy, I don't want you to ever say sorry to me again – 95% of the sorrys in my team come from women and I'm quite sure they're not making 95% of the mistakes!" Younger women can be self-effacing and immediately start with sorry. It's such a powerful word and should not be overused.

I have seen ideas being ignored because the person is too quiet. Unless you have a boss who's very thoughtful about inviting different voices into the room, women and men can be ignored. Often those quieter ones might take a bit more time, but they have valuable input.

Women are generally thoughtful about how much confidence they show because it's more easily seen as arrogance than with men. A confident woman sometimes has difficultly dealing with men who feel threatened.

If there's a bad fit with a boss or job, then women very quickly lose self-confidence. I've seen this with younger women I've mentored. They lose their spark and start doubting everything they do. Sometimes building back their confidence is just a matter of believing in them and reminding them that they're really good.

If a job is not a good fit, it's time to think through what you want, start talking to people, making connections.

Life is too short to stay in a role where you can't be your best.

SANDY GRIFFITHS

Sandy was most recently marketing and innovation director at Diageo. As well as being an immensely colourful character, she's a dynamic, inspirational and results-orientated leader.

During our interview, we discussed her love of everything to do with marketing, the career challenges of becoming a mum, the importance of EQ and compromise, and how she loves to empower people.

We have written up part of the interview as one of our Inspiring Stories: When Madiba met Simba (see page 128).

HOW DID YOU GET INTO MARKETING?

As a South African of colour, marketing wasn't presented as an option. You could be a teacher, lawyer, doctor or accountant. I did finance at university but hated it. Then I went through psychometric testing and was told, "You're not going to be successful as an accountant – you need to be in advertising or marketing." This was when I decided to join 3M and was lucky enough to be sent to St Paul, Minnesota Innovation Centre for training.

So, I learned the 3M way of innovating. They had 86,000 skus and only innovation business cases that ensured a return of investment within three years would see the light of day, so we were trained on crafting these business cases. There was a formula to it, and I LOVED it. I eventually became the youngest marketing manager of colour in South Africa.

I love gathering insights, understanding what drives consumer behaviour, and how that translates to how they purchase and consume. If you are smart enough, you can innovate and market to create that desire, or you can take an insight and just amplify it and make people more aware of that's what they want.

I love how marketing has changed and evolved. Occasions, need states, geographies – how one consumption occasion changes across geographies. I love that immersion into the culture that allows you to see a different consumer view. Marketing is such an evolving model that I'm never going to be bored with it. It is even more interesting as we watch new generations' consumption patterns, not just of products and services but media and communication as well.

WHAT HAVE BEEN THE MILESTONES IN YOUR CAREER?
It wasn't a long road to get to a senior position. I was head-hunted into Colgate Palmolive, then to Revlon, then Pepsico.

The biggest challenge was when I fell pregnant. I decided to take a year out – then it was a struggle to get back onto the ladder.

If you step back on the same rung, it's fair. When you have to take a step down, it's unfair. When I went back to work, I left one organization and started with another in a different industry, nonalcoholic drinks. All those guys on the rung above me didn't have as much marketing experience as I did – that was really difficult.

Coca-Cola was a fast moving and dynamic culture. I was learning and travelling a lot, and the biggest challenge was balancing work and private life. Coca-Cola was very accommodating in understanding I was the newly divorced mother of a young child and allowed my daughter to travel with me when it was necessary. Flexibility is critical. I think a lot of organizations preach it, but don't practice it.

When I became a mother, my IQ may not have had a major step change, but my EQ certainly did! Before I had my daughter, I was less empathetic, more about ME. After I had her, I was more empathetic and more about US. And my leadership skills grew dramatically.

WHAT WERE THE CHALLENGES YOU FACED AS A WOMAN OF COLOUR?

Generally, the challenges were less about being a woman of colour, more about being a woman. In South Africa, however, it tended to be more about race than gender.

My last job was in a male-dominated industry with men who had been in the industry forever. The first challenge was being a female and the second was being from outside the category. As a woman from a different category, they employ you because you'll bring diversity of thinking, but the moment you make a suggestion about doing things differently, you get it thrown back in your face, "No, that's not the way we do that here."

If I take senior leadership in Africa as an example, 90% of the time I'd be the only female on a business call. It never bothered me, but the question raised was, "Why am I the only female here?" What I experienced was my male colleagues talking over me – it was almost as if they tolerated me, but never took me seriously. Don't employ females if you're not going to listen to their point of view.

Another challenge I faced was women themselves! Some women think they have to imitate men to be taken seriously – they are rude, brash and have no empathy. They forget their natural traits because they think it will not get them where they need to be. I believe in authenticity, so I'm going to just be me. Whether at home or work, I'm the same person. As female leaders, we are sometimes our worst enemies by not empowering other women.

WOMEN SHOULD NOT ATTEMPT TO BE MEDIOCRE.

– SANDY GRIFFITHS

WHAT ARE YOU MOST PROUD OF?

Besides delivering the business agenda, I'm proud to see the success of the people I have coached and mentored. I'm most proud of the teams that I've built to deliver the business agenda.

I continually strive for achievement of my personal purpose, which is, "Leaving it better than I found it," and I have been able to empower people along the way – that's what I'd love to be known for.

WHAT DO WOMEN UNIQUELY BRING TO MARKETING?

Mostly humility and a sense of sharing! The men try to outdo each other, but the women will undersell themselves. For example, a woman would say, "I've done this – I hope this is what you're looking for." Whereas a man would say, "You're gonna love this." I would have to reassure the females of how great they were, whereas the men would not see where there were gaps, and if you pointed it out, you had to be extremely diplomatic.

The sharing culture is also less prevalent in males. For example, I had two heads of functions in my marketing team. The female would compliment the male on a great job and would seek to understand how he did it, but he rarely shared his knowledge. She, on the other hand, would go out of her way to take him through her expertise, share her presentations and then be hurt that he did not reciprocate.

So, it's that humility versus arrogance, sharing versus not sharing.

At my level, what I didn't enjoy about my male counterparts was the lack of authenticity and honesty. Feedback was very rarely honest and face-to-face. Feedback is a gift whether it's positive or negative. My male counterparts thought that if they shared the glory, they gave away their power. For many men, it's a battle for power and they believe that unshared knowledge is power.

HOW DO YOU FEEL ABOUT THE FUTURE OF WOMEN IN MARKETING?

When I look at Millennials and Gen Z, they see less difference whether it's gender, race or culture, and I feel hugely optimistic. I believe we are evolving as a society. I see how my daughter interacts at uni – how everyone's individual contribution is appreciated, nobody talks above anyone else and everyone is respected for what they bring to the table.

I am the eternal optimist. I'd like to not have the conversation of male/female or black/white – you're either great at what you do or not. We need to be more tolerant of differences and see it as something valuable; we need to be more open and appreciative of different cultures.

There's always going to be inequity, depending on how you grew up. But as society changes and women are educated and enter the workforce, I believe it will change. Now, women have to go out and earn a living as much as men do, so there is the question – well, if I have to go out to work, then you have to participate in the home. It also comes down to the strength of character of both men and women.

I have a controversial point of view – and my female colleagues will probably batter me! Women must learn to draw the lines on where they can compete and win – they must play to their strengths. Women should not attempt to be mediocre; they should attempt to overachieve, but when this happens, it needs to be acknowledged by both male and female leaders.

This whole equality discussion becomes a bit of an exercise in futility. We should be choosing careers that we love and where we can excel, rather than because it's a male-dominated sector.

At the end of the day, we must believe that we all bring something unique to the table.

ELENA MARCHENKO

Elena is global category director at Arla in Denmark. She is immensely proud of the Arla company, which stands for bringing health and natural goodness to consumers, securing a fair milk price for their cooperative of farmers, and a commitment to sustainability for a stronger planet.

During our interview, we talked about her experience of working across European markets, her personal 3 Ps – professionalism, possibilities and people – and why *Alice in Wonderland* is the book all marketers should read.

HOW DID YOU GET INTO A CAREER IN MARKETING?

I'm Russian, and marketing was a new thing at the time of my deciding what direction I wanted to take with my education. I studied finance and economics at university in St Petersburg and marketing was a small part of the course, but for me it was the 'cherry on the cake.' I thought marketing was super interesting, but I couldn't see how I would be able to apply it in real life.

Then, in my second job, I had to deal with marketing and discovered that out of the whole company, I had the best sense about consumer behaviour. Suddenly, I became an expert and loved it! It may sound naïve, but it's my true belief that marketing is all about making the world a bit better. Brands are not just products; brands make the world a bit more colourful; they make life more interesting and exciting; and when brands have strong beliefs, they can be powerful forces for good.

I switched into marketing and ever since I've been continually learning. Marketing is not like a science that is set in stone and you have clear rules and laws; it is always developing. There are always new challenges and new ways of thinking. That's why l like it so much.

Marketing is also so diverse – you need to apply all parts of your brain and all your interests. It spans both analytical and creative, it can be about tactical solutions as well as high-level strategy – all in one role. You have to apply all your different skills and switch from one to the other really fast. Within just a couple hours you can be discussing the data from the research, working out how to turn it into the insight, making a decision on the right Pantone colour for design, creating the business case and then you have to turn into creative mode.

WHAT LED TO YOUR SUCCESS IN MARKETING?

If you're brave enough and strongly believe you can make a difference, it will help you grow and build your career.

Being a Russian marketer in the European market was more of a challenge for me than being a woman. At that time (almost a decade ago) Russia was perceived to be a 'newcomer' in world-class marketing. When I came into the European environment, the question was asked, "What can you, as a Russian, bring to the table?" In marketing terms, Russia only started to exist 20 years ago, but now the market is super strong.

That challenge helped me because I had to prove every time that I was a professional and really good at what I was doing. I'm thankful for that. It kept me on my toes all the time and helped me perform at my best.

DID YOU ENCOUNTER ANY BARRIERS SPECIFIC TO BEING A WOMAN IN MARKETING?

When I started out in marketing, I knew so many brand and marketing managers who were strong and successful women in medium-tier positions. However, the more senior you get, the more it becomes a man's world.

My observations are that men are better at *projecting* the power, showing ambition, pushing themselves forward; they're 'aggressive' in a positive way, and they openly say, "I'm keen to lead, I can be a leader, I'm ambitious, I seek power." This is perceived by society as normal for a man. If a woman shows the same behaviour, she's perceived as too 'aggressive' in a negative way. Although the world has changed significantly over the last 20 years, we still have deep perceptions that women can't show this dominant behaviour. And this holds us back.

For a woman to get into a high-level position, she needs to demonstrate she is a strong personality, show direction and leadership, but at the same time she shouldn't do it in the same way as men because it is perceived differently. Women need to navigate it carefully to get the balance right. You have to stay strong, and you have to bang your fist on the table sometimes; but realize this may be perceived as normal for men, but not for women.

As a woman you have to be flexible, but you also have to stick to your beliefs and decisions. It's important to present the supporting facts and rationale for your thoughts and ideas (even while for men this is sometimes not even discussed). Most importantly, you have to stay true to yourself. You have to say, "That's me, my personality, my beliefs, I'm not delineating from it."

It has changed a lot in the last six to seven years of my career. I see a lot of admiration for women in leadership positions; they are appreciated for bringing diversity of thinking. It's great to see it is becoming a battle that it is possible to win.

WHAT CHALLENGES DOES PARENTING BRING IN THE MARKETING WORLD?

When I became a parent, I didn't have difficulties because of the great support from my husband and then from the Danish society. My daughter is now a teenager, so she's not seeking my attention – it's more a question of getting her into of the room to talk to her parents!

In Scandinavia there's a good support system and positive perception of mothers who work. Here 'family comes first,' and it's absolutely normal to say you can't go to an important meeting because you have an open day at school with your child. I have colleagues who leave at 3pm to collect kids, but if they need to do something, they'll pick it up when the kids have gone to bed at 8pm. Everything we agreed on gets done. They're not compromising their work; they're just balancing their life, and they're usually super-efficient.

However, having had the experience of working in Russia and Germany, it's not the same situation in all countries. All countries are similar in that women legally have equal rights, but expectations about women differ. In Germany, a woman in my team was on maternity leave, and when discussing her plans for returning to work, she said she would love to come back after one year, but it would not be perceived well, as there was still the perception that you're not a good mother if you leave your child before they are three years old. I was really surprised and thought it so old-fashioned.

IF NOBODY WILL
CHALLENGE OR THINK
DIFFERENTLY, NOTHING WILL
EVER CHANGE. YOU HAVE TO
STOP SOMETIMES AND THINK
DIFFERENTLY TO MAKE
A DIFFERENCE.

— ELENA MARCHENKO

WHAT ARE YOU MOST PROUD OF IN YOUR CAREER?

The bigger things, where I can make a difference.

When I look back, I'm proud of my ability to stay strong during the storm – to become a solid rock for my team and for my company, not to go into panic mode, keep the vision, keep the direction, be agile and keep the business going.

Most of my roles have involved turning businesses around, where the brand needs to be reinvigorated. When I started working on the Tuborg brand globally, it was in decline. The situation was very tough, and it had to be changed fast. When I left that position, the brand was healthy, growing, and it was bigger than Carlsberg!

I can't say that was my achievement alone – it was a team achievement.

YOU TALK ABOUT THE IMPORTANCE OF THE 3 PS. WHAT DO YOU MEAN BY THAT?

I was at a leadership development course and they asked the question, "How would you describe what's important for you?" I said it comes down to 3Ps.

The first is professionalism and by this I mean the ability to do your job on a very high level and always continue to develop yourself, and never believe you're the expert. This is important for myself as well as what I'm looking for from people in my team.

The second is possibilities. You need to find the possibilities to develop business and believe that they exist. If nobody will challenge or think differently, nothing will ever change. Who would have thought that a phone could also be a camera and a laptop? Or that cars could be electric? Things happen because people challenge convention.

The third is people. Without people, without their talents, ideas, their beliefs and energy, nothing will be possible.

TELL US ABOUT THE ALICE IN WONDERLAND STORY

The CEO of a company I was working for proclaimed that the best book for any marketer or businessperson is *Alice in Wonderland*!

He went on to use quotes from the book that supported his statements. For example, when talking about the importance of being ahead of the curve, he used the quote, "It takes all the running you can do, to keep in the same place. If you want to get somewhere else, you must run at least twice as fast as that!"

It was a great presentation and showed how sometimes you need to think differently to make a difference.

HARRIET DE SWIET

Harriet is Managing Director APAC at Brand Learning, which is now part of Accenture. She was advised by a friend of her aunt, who was a senior executive at P&G in Mexico, that her skills would suit marketing. She pursued a successful career client-side with Unilever, British Airways and Bupa before switching to consultancy.

During our interview, we talked about the importance of understanding both people and commerce, the extraordinary female leaders who have inspired her, and the great opportunities for women in marketing.

HOW DID YOU GET INTO A CAREER IN MARKETING?

Before going to university, in my year off, I worked in conference management and decided I wanted to do that. I then went to uni, where I did a languages degree. In my third year, which I did in Mexico, I did a marketing elective because I thought it sounded interesting. That Christmas, still in Mexico, I was invited to stay with an old friend of my aunt's. Martha Lombera, a senior exec at P&G, was there. She saw my interest in marketing and suggested that I should aim 'bigger' than conference management and go into marketing. She thought I had all the attributes required.

What interested me then, and still does, is the combination of psychology and commerce. Marketing is about people, and I've always been interested in people and what makes them tick, but marketing also brings the challenge of ensuring that what you do makes commercial sense. It's not about fooling people into buying your product or service once; it's about building brands that people will come back to time and time again.

WHAT HAS BEEN YOUR EXPERIENCE AS A WOMAN IN MARKETING AND RISE TO A SENIOR POSITION?

I've been privileged to have extraordinary female leaders around me throughout my career, both as colleagues and clients.

When I started out at Birdseye, I worked with and learned from both great marketers and astute commercial leaders. At British Airways, I learned what courage looks like, what passenger centricity looks like, and how to lead large teams of people.

Bupa was very different culturally, and I suppose I got a bit stuck in the middle management layer. My brand role was really a pure comms role, so a very different role, more focused, and very different to the role I aspired to fulfil.

I decided I should move on and set out to find somewhere much smaller, where I could feel the impact of what I was doing.

That is why I joined Brand Learning, where I was surrounded by extraordinary leaders, both men and women, and have continued to learn, grow and be inspired.

WHAT ARE YOU MOST PROUD OF?

Courage isn't always taking a leap of faith, sometimes it is knowing when to say "stop" or "no." At Unilever, I was part of the first Frozen Food Innovation Centre. One project involved trying to make microwaveable fishfingers, but despite the best efforts of the team, we couldn't get them to be crispy in the way our customers wanted. I had to pull the project, and I'm proud of the courage I showed in making that call.

That was an example of my commercial sensibility, but when at British Airways, one of things I'm most proud of related to understanding people. I was part of a team that unlocked the insight behind what frequent flyers were looking for. Interestingly, while these customers were mainly businessmen, what we discovered was that they genuinely had emotional equity in the airline, a 'relationship' with the brand. We realized that they cared about the airline even if they were not flying, or flying with a competitor, and we needed to match that emotional commitment. It really helped us develop the way we looked after our very important Gold Card holders.

I'm proud of my ability to adapt, change and grow, and this is perhaps reflected in what I have achieved since moving into consultancy. I've learned to see things from a different perspective – I was no longer the 'client'. I'm proud of the relationships I've built with our clients and have worked hard to understand their 'worlds' and what they each need to deliver.

WHAT ARE THE BENEFITS AND DRAWBACKS OF BEING A WOMAN IN MARKETING?

I think that historically marketing has been attractive to women, in a similar way to HR. It's welcoming and inclusive, especially client-side, and it's much easier for a woman to thrive in a marketing role than in tech, for example.

In male-dominated arenas, it can be more difficult for a woman, and I've seen a little of that at Bupa and at Accenture, where regularly I am the only women in the meeting. Accenture has an annual seminar for everyone who's joined as an MD, and this year, of the 350 people at the seminar, only 30 to 40 were women. No wonder it's something they and I want to change.

On the agency side, especially advertising, digital and media, it's still a male culture; there are still old ad men knocking around the corridors, and some of those old habits and attitudes are prevalent among the digital tech guys too!

Collaboration is important to getting things done in marketing today and, in general, women find that easier. Rather than taking a command-and-control approach, women are good at building networks, making connections and influencing people, so it's a good time for women from that perspective.

Marketers also need to be commercial, and it's wholly wrong to say that's only ever a male domain. A lot of the female marketing leaders I admire have been grounded in the commercial reality.

One of my roles is Vice Chair of the Marketing Society in Southeast Asia. Our membership is 50/50 women and men. However, there are several problems for women in marketing in Asia; in particular, marketing is a relatively new profession and is not a career people aspire to. Parents want their daughters to be lawyers, doctors or engineers, to go into the 'traditional' professions. We need to consider how we build the reputation of marketing as a profession in this part of the world; how do we make it attractive and aspirational and develop future CEOs who might be either men or women.

Marketing leadership needs to evolve to better build future leaders who can get to the C-suite. When I started my career as an assistant brand manager at Unilever, I was basically the MD of a sku (a single stock-keeping unit – a product). You worked your way up to a leadership position and you knew how to do the jobs beneath you. That's not how it works now. There are specialized micro niches, so you have people who are leading functions with zero knowledge of how others are working. It begs the question, how will we move people up out of their specialisms to be leaders, and will micro specialisms favour men or women?

RATHER THAN TAKING A COMMAND-AND-CONTROL APPROACH, WOMEN ARE GOOD AT BUILDING NETWORKS, MAKING CONNECTIONS AND INFLUENCING PEOPLE, SO IT'S A GOOD TIME FOR WOMEN FROM THAT PERSPECTIVE.

– HARRIET DE SWIET

WHAT DO WOMEN UNIQUELY BRING TO MARKETING?

If I think about the marketers I've worked with, it's noticeable that many of the women are better at the deep insight work; thinking way beyond the obvious, showing empathy and curiosity. Women have intuition and it takes courage to realize it, point to it and do something about it.

Courage and bravery is something many women bring too.

When Nina Bibby redesigned the logo at IHG and moved to H, it was a real challenge. There was a real sense of, "Am I destroying decades of the brand or driving it forward?" It was a courageous decision.

Lynette Pang, CEO of Singapore Tourist Board, realized that STB needed a new brand purpose and positioning that would pull Singapore apart from its competitors. She understood it's a small country and therefore it needed to be very targeted. They took an idea, amplified it and developed it into 'Passion Made Possible,' which was courageous because passion was a potentially divisive concept. Some Singaporeans didn't feel they were 'passionate.' Lynette worked hard to find an interpretation of passion that was right for Singapore both within the country and beyond.

For both Lynette and Nina, it didn't matter how much research they did; ultimately, it came down to their own judgment, not whether 53% of customers liked it or not. Like me, they believe that most marketing research should be for guidance, not decision making. Ultimately, it comes down to a mix of the evidence, your judgment, your experience and your intuition.

However, having said all this, my worry with your question is it's potentially damning to men; why wouldn't at least some men be able to bring the same things to marketing? From my experience, some do.

Personally, I hope the future is about getting and celebrating the right balance of capabilities and character in our future marketing leaders whether they are men or women.

Marketing is about meeting people's needs profitably and the gender of marketers shouldn't be an issue.

SALLY BIBB

Sally is the founder of and a director at Engaging Minds, an author and public speaker. Her specialisms are transforming organizations, customer service, employee engagement and organizational change. Engaging Minds works in private companies, hospitals and prisons and clients include Starbucks, the AA, Cunard, EY, HMCTS (Her Majesty's Courts and Tribunals Service), the NHS, the Scottish Government and Sodexo Justice Services.

She has worked in a variety of fields, starting in the telecomms sector for BT and Cable and Wireless to and became a director at The Economist Group before starting Engaging Minds.

She has written and co-authored eight books, the latest of which is *The Strengths Workbook: An eight-week programme to discover your strengths.*

In our interview, we talked about how anger can create something positive, how prejudices can give you strength, and her interest in the debate about capitalism and whether GDP is the right measure.

WHAT LED YOU TO WHERE YOU ARE NOW?

I've always been interested in people and their stories. Looking back, every job I've ever done has had a strong element of 'people.'

I'm also interested in how you tackle injustices and things that are wrong with organizations, as well as boosting the things that are right. When people are not treated properly, it really gets my goat. I always aim to make a positive difference in organizations.

YOU TALK ABOUT 'GETTING YOUR GOAT.' ANGER CAN BE A POSITIVE FORCE FOR CHANGE. IS IT ABOUT TIME WOMEN GOT ANGRIER?

It's something that women aren't supposed to be. But when things are wrong and unjust, that can create anger, and anger can create something positive and that in turn can create more energy. You see it in politics, you see it everywhere. When men get angry, people seem to accept it. When women get angry, they get trolled. It's a stark contrast.

I hope that the #MeToo movement will be a force for good, but the unconscious stereotypes of what men and women should be are so deep. It definitely has the potential to be a big moment in history for equality because it is bringing things out in the open and creating a much-needed challenge.

WHAT HAVE BEEN THE CHALLENGES YOU'VE FACED IN YOUR CAREER?

In the early days, as I was establishing myself, it was to do with assumptions about a quiet, working-class girl. I once found a note in my HR file from a manager to my boss about a promotion I'd just got which said something like, 'She's too quiet, she won't be able to stand the challenge.' Thankfully, my boss backed me up, and I was very successful in the job.

When I got the job at The Economist, my boss said one of the reasons she brought me in was because, "You've got the common touch." I was being compared to private school/ Oxbridge educated people and she saw the positive in that.

None of those prejudices made me angry – they gave me strength, made me more determined, more resilient. You have to have a tough skin. I didn't want to be put in a box.

As a woman, I'm uncomfortable about blowing my own trumpet. A lot of men don't have that problem. Social media is very interesting. When I post on social media, I sometimes think, "My god, does this sound like awful showing off?" But how do you learn if the women you admire don't blow their own trumpets? I think to be a role model in an active way is important; you need to talk about what matters to you and what you've achieved, and recognize that it will benefit others.

THINKING ABOUT SMALL BUSINESSES LIKE YOURSELF, DO YOU THINK THERE ARE MORE WOMEN ENTREPRENEURS WHO ARE DOING THINGS DIFFERENTLY NOW?

What interests me is the debate about capitalism and whether GDP is the right measure.

Katrin Jakobsdottir, Prime Minister of Iceland, has teamed up with Nicola Sturgeon, Scottish First Minister and Jacinda Ardern, Prime Minister of New Zealand, to promote a wellbeing agenda because they recognize that GDP is very limiting as a measure of success.

I was invited by EY to enter their Business of the Year Award. I looked at the shortlisted people and it was all about huge growth. We were invited to enter because EY wanted to consider entrants for whom social impact was as important, if not more important, than growth.

WHAT DO WOMEN BRING UNIQUELY TO BUSINESS AND MARKETING?

In my world, we want to make sure we make an impact. One of my strengths is conscientiousness. I just can't let it go until we make sure we've done our bit and made a difference. Most of the women I hang out with also want to make that sort of difference. I am not saying that the men don't, but I have different conversations with them.

When I talk about making an impact, I mean social impact rather than financial impact. That's what makes me happy.

The women I admire come from all sorts of different backgrounds and are doing different things. Many are leaving the corporate world to set up their own businesses, which means they have to learn fast about all aspects of running a business.

Many of the women I know are always in a process of development. I too try to make myself better. Women will try things, experiment, make themselves more vulnerable throughout their lives.

I think I know more women who are willing to make an idiot of themselves. I know some men like that, but not so many.

I did a talk in Madrid – in Spanish. Of the people I told, nearly all the men replied with, "You must be crazy." The women said, "Oh my god, that's fantastic, you're so brave."

GOING FORWARD, WHAT ARE THE CHALLENGES THAT WOMEN IN BUSINESS FACE AND ARE THEY DIFFERENT FROM MEN'S?

The atmosphere is calling for doing things differently, so it's a good time for women. The female characteristics we talked about, like conscientiousness and wanting to make a social impact, are needed and more valued now. The whole thing about GDP versus social impact. We still face a deep gender bias in society and that probably won't change anytime soon. I think probably for men it's about seeing how things are changing, getting onboard with supporting genuine equality in the workplace and being adaptable to the changes themselves.

AS A WOMAN, I'M UNCOMFORTABLE ABOUT BLOWING MY OWN TRUMPET. A LOT OF MEN DON'T HAVE THAT PROBLEM.

– SALLY BIBB

CATHERINE GRAINGER

Catherine has spent 19 years of her career at 3M in a broad range of marketing roles. She now shares her expertise in marketing training across Europe, the Middle East and Africa.

During the interview, we talked about learning her skills, marketing an incontinence product, the importance of empathy and gut instinct, how she manages her work/life balance, the power of networking and how small talk is actually big talk.

HOW DID YOU GET INTO A CAREER IN MARKETING?

It wasn't planned! I liked being creative and I had a way with words, so initially wanted to be a journalist. After graduating in communication studies, I got a job as a sales and marketing coordinator for a small multimedia company. I enjoyed the buzz of the marketing side, creating compelling content, arranging exhibitions, PR, speaking to journalists.

Then I went to 3M; I thought the job description described my capabilities perfectly, plus they made lots of cool stuff.

WHAT WERE YOUR EARLY SUCCESSES?

In the early days, 3M launched a product called Cavilon™ No Sting Barrier Film. It's a skin barrier product that protects the skin against bodily fluids from chronic wounds or incontinence – not particularly glamorous! There was nothing like it in the market, so we had a blank slate.

We ran a campaign with district nurses, which gave us huge exposure and was a clear lesson on how to grow a brand.

We then launched another product in the range, Cavilon™ Durable Barrier Cream, and that taught me all about positioning, about creating compelling yet differentiating value propositions, so that both products could find their own niche. We made the distinction for the two products – broken skin for the film, intact skin for the cream. The communication with district nurses was really clear. We used case studies and demo aids to create the story. We grew the two products from £0 to a multimillion-pound business and it became known as THE skin protectant range.

We've now got lots of competitors but still hold our position in the market.

WHAT HELPED YOUR SUCCESS IN MARKETING AT 3M?

First, developing empathetic skills and thinking about the customer. It's important to put yourself into their shoes, understand their pain points, spend time with them and never assume you know it all.

Second, creating the balance of rigour and creativity. In the early days, it was more straightforward, as you could use your gut instinct. Data can be overwhelming, and people get lost in it; too much reliance on it means you can lose the ability to build a good understanding and have confidence in your intuition.

Third, thinking creatively about approaches. I've brought more creativity into the strategic marketing process through workshop facilitation, war gaming, competitor analysis and customer journey. As an organization, we can be serious and process driven, so it's important to inject empathy and creativity.

SMALL TALK IS ACTUALLY BIG TALK.

– CATHERINE GRAINGER

HAVE THERE BEEN CONSTRAINTS AS A WOMAN IN MARKETING?

I've been fortunate – any barriers have been self-imposed! 3M is a good company to work for, as it is very encouraging of women in the workplace and women's leadership is a big thing. They want to encourage more women into senior positions, but the number of women tails off at a certain job level; a level at which is more comfortable to manage when you also have a family.

A big challenge is how to manage work/life balance after having children. For me, it's the law of diminishing returns – the demands on me would become too much if I pushed higher. The double burden of handling kids and housework can often fall more to women than men and that's a challenge.

Also, if I want to take my foot off the gas for a couple years, how do I manage work? I've never had a career plan. My career path has been spontaneous rather than saying, "this is what I want to happen."

It's easier as children get older. It's much more full-on when they're young, as they need you more to be there. The tricky thing is trying to do it all – sometimes that means working 9am to 3pm then 8pm to 10pm. A drawback is that you can sacrifice the 'me' time, then you end up frazzled and everyone suffers. I deliberately worked part-time and stopped chasing promotions at 3M for about six years while my kids were little. I don't regret it for a moment, but nor do I judge mums who work full time, or those who continue to perform well and get promotions. All power to them!

Tech is an enabling factor, and it has helped me take on my current job. You need a high degree of trust and clear objectives if you're working from home. The debate has moved on from presenteeism; the flexibility that working remotely offers has enabled me to embrace my new role as marketing training manager. The role can be full-on, especially when I'm out of the country, but it's very fulfilling. When I'm home I can start work at 7am, then be finished by 5pm – it's a great balance.

WHAT ARE THE CHARACTERISTICS AND TRAITS THAT WOMEN BRING MORE THAN MEN IN MARKETING?

That's difficult to answer without generalizing, but I would say that women are better at empathy, at getting the most out of teams and recognizing the challenges they are facing. Women tend to be better at building empathy for the customer – how and why they are thinking in the way they do. Men are more transactional. Women look at the layer below – at unconscious needs. There's a step change if you immerse yourself in the customer's world.

Characteristics such as authenticity and seeing the bigger picture help you succeed – after all, work is only part of what we do. Understanding and connecting with a life outside of work makes for a better person.

Work is not just about driving results. Teams of people will have good and bad days, so you need to understand what makes them tick. Showing a genuine interest gets the most out of people.

In my EMEA role, I spend most of my day on Skype calls. If used badly, it's a soulless experience, so we spend more time getting to know our colleagues. For example, when working with a colleague from Germany, we shared Google maps on our screen and showed each other where we lived and the interesting places to visit. It helped to make that connection that you get more easily face to face. Building virtual connections is a critical skill in today's workplace.

A major barrier for women is the perception of networking. Some women still have the old-fashioned view that networking is about a round of golf or drinking – the old boys club. That's not what networking is. There are more female events, but networking should be about everyone.

Networking is important in 3M as it is a matrix organization, so you need to connect the dots; push yourself outside your comfort zone and find out about people. Women are good at talking and getting to know people. We all need to be more deliberate with networking – especially if looking for your next job move.

Small talk is good for building relationships – it's not so small when it's about connectivity and bonding. Everyone has a memory problem, so I make notes about people – their kids names, where they went on holiday, etc. I put them into PowerPoint notes and look back on them before the next meeting. Doing that is really powerful because it's hugely important to people – it's actually big talk.

2012 –
THE PRESENT
(MILLENNIALS):
#ACTIVISM

Our Millennial Wonder Women entered their careers in the 21st century with the backdrop of the fourth wave of feminism, characterized by a focus on the empowerment of women and intersectionality, which identifies advantages and disadvantages that are felt by people due to a combination of factors (e.g. gender, sex, race, class, sexuality, religion).

With the internet at our collective fingertips, it is possible to share ideas, information and movements faster than ever before. The internet fuelled the fire behind the #MeToo movement, and the Everyday Sexism Project, where women worldwide can share their stories of sexual harassment and workplace discrimination.

Fourth-wave feminism argues for equal pay for equal work, and that the equal opportunities sought for girls and women should extend also to boys and men to overcome gender norms (for example, by expressing emotions and feelings freely, expressing themselves physically as they wish, and to be engaged parents to their children).

In the workplace, there's a much stronger drive for diversity, more flexible working patterns and company cultures, which embrace both male and female characteristics.

JOSSIE MORRISON

Like many Millennials, Jossie Morrison expects a fast-track career on her own terms. She's happy to change direction to follow her passions and the lifestyle she wants. She started her marketing journey in brand consultancy, then onto Waitrose, where she was one of eight selected from over 2,000 for their leadership programme. An opportunity to live in Bermuda led her to set up her own business, The Brand Bulb.

During our interview, we discussed the importance of asking big questions, why marketing should have equal recognition with finance, how thinking about the customer leads to success, how today's generation of men seem so different from those before, her strong views on what is holding women back, and why a focus purely on female equality improvement is no longer the way forward.

HOW DID YOU DECIDE ON A CAREER IN MARKETING?

My decision to focus on marketing mirrored that of my degree choice, theology and religious studies. I was good at debating, articulate, loved language and asking questions, as well as considering different points of view.

I also love selling stuff. We have a family retail business, so I'd spent time on a shop floor for years. I adore chatting with customers, solving their problems on the spot, influencing a sale and feeling the money going through the till!

IF MUMS AND DADS
ARE BETTER SUPPORTED
IN THEIR WORK AND
WITH THEIR FAMILIES,
COMPANIES ALL OVER THE
WORLD WILL THRIVE.

– JOSSIE MORRISON

WHAT LED TO YOUR SUCCESS?

I'm not sure I am successful yet! One of my bug bears is that marketing and creative skills are seen as 'fluffy.' When I first started working in brand consultancy, my friends, especially the guys who worked in finance or law, asked, "What do you do? Just design logos?"

I told them it's business planning from a creative point of view and it's just as important as financial planning. I always feel like the people with the financial brain have the last word; to me, that's not as it should be – a company's finances, operations and communications need to be equally respected for it to truly thrive. Of course, profit is the goal but all too often marketing can be disrespected by people with different skill sets. I've always tried to think about championing customer delight as the best way of delivering the biggest possible profits. To me, cutting corners with the customer might save a buck in the short term, but it costs a fortune down the road.

I never enjoyed maths and science, which for a long time left me feeling like my success would be limited, as I'm not a whizz with the numbers. It's taken time and some fantastic mentors to help me focus on my strengths instead of my weaknesses. Asking questions and delegating help me get around not being the best in the room with a spreadsheet. When I'm operating at my absolute best, I'm motivating other people, making connections and figuring out a plan that's based on measurable, realistic goals.

I HAVE HEARD THAT YOUR WAITROSE LEADERSHIP SCHEME INTAKE WAS 100% FEMALE. HOW DID THAT COME ABOUT?

It was a rigorous interview process. They wanted the best people, and we happened to all be women. They selected purely on merit. I thought that was awesome.

Supermarkets have historically been quite male-dominated environments from a management perspective. I thrive on that challenge because I'm competitive, but I had to be aware of being judged and accept that I'm blonde, I have a posh voice, and there was resentment toward us all on the scheme not because we were women, but because we were managing people with a lot more experience than us. It was a tough but formative experience. I realized that leading a team isn't necessarily having the answers myself but playing to the individual strengths of everyone in that team.

I helped set up a gender discussion network for Waitrose and John Lewis, which was a great profile builder. People just assumed it was a women's network, so we worked hard to make sure loads of men attended, especially people with senior positions.

IT'S INTERESTING HOW YOU HIGHLIGHT THAT GENDER DISCUSSIONS ARE NOT JUST A FEMALE ISSUE.

It's not a very feminist thing to say, but loads of women do everyone else a disservice by whining. They have to stop and have a two-way gender conversation.

Women constantly bashing the current generation of men won't fix the problem. My peers who are men are not part of the problem; today's generation are so much more involved in equality and childcare. It's a realistic hope that my daughter won't know a single man who hasn't changed a nappy or taken paternity leave!

WHAT ARE YOU MOST PROUD OF IN YOUR CAREER?

I was proud of doing well at The Value Engineers, especially when I got promoted to consultant. I thought, "Yes, perhaps I can do this after all." When I look back at the collective projects I worked on, I feel proud that I was trusted to take on major parts of projects – like when I was sent out to Mumbai on a British Airways project.

Getting onto the Waitrose leadership scheme was life-changing. I hadn't believed that a big company like that would take me seriously. It also made me hungry for feedback – both good and bad!

In Bermuda, I was proud of just finding a job initially – I needed to move there for my husband's job – and now I'm proud of reinventing myself in setting up my own business to suit our life here better.

Since 'going it alone,' I've also been incredibly proud of being accepted by, and becoming a director of, Hoxby. I couldn't believe that a global freelancing collective would take me seriously, and I've learned so much from them in terms of the future of working, thinking in a more agile way about how to get things done and the power of community.

WHAT CHARACTERISTICS DO WOMEN UNIQUELY BRING TO MARKETING?

SO many! I know we're not meant to generalize about the differences between men and women, but I think that women are naturally more curious about other people, which is the heart of marketing.

Sadly, however, I think that women still hold themselves back more than men, myself included. Also, for some reason I always felt that beating a man at something – to a promotion, a competition, whatever – was more satisfying than beating a woman at something; for some reason, being a girl beating a boy felt more surprising. That needs to change!

Women take things more personally than men. I believe that men are better at compartmentalizing and self-promotion, regardless of industry. Men don't put themselves down as much and aren't as terrified of saying they're good at things.

I'm at that age when kids – having them, not having them and then managing work around them – are a recurrent conversation. That's also made me think about what we as mums bring to work – in no way meaning to do the dads out there a disservice (my husband is phenomenally hands-on with our daughter and arguably more instinctive than me about what she wants!).

The sheer experience of childbirth and physical recovery forces women to develop a natural resilience they might not have had before. That, to me, is a huge strength in the workplace, i.e. the ability to adapt and surprise oneself. If mums and dads are better supported in their work and with their families, companies all over the world will thrive. The Hoxby Collective champions this strongly, and I think is doing fantastic work on that front.

WHAT ARE THE ADVANTAGES OF BEING A WOMAN IN MARKETING?

As women, we get to position ourselves with our style – how we dress, how we look. It sounds shallow, but I think that's a huge advantage that women have in the workplace as we get to send messages to our teams, clients and prospects about our confidence, our values and our personality before we've even opened our mouths. For men, it's far more difficult to position themselves aesthetically.

Women look to enjoy their jobs more than men. They choose careers based on what they will enjoy over money. Women bring a lot more passion; that's harsh on men, but it's true.

Men think, "What am I good at? What pays well? What's my long-term career?" Men have to take big decisions about financial responsibility, especially when kids are on the way. In most relationships I know, including my own, it's the man who is the main breadwinner still; that isn't necessarily a bad thing, but we need to give men credit for the unsaid societal expectation that their careers are a must have, not a nice to have.

I have lost count of the times I was asked, during pregnancy and after the birth of my daughter, if I was planning to go back to work. My husband wasn't asked that once, which has made me reconsider male and female work equality. If he were also asked that question, it might make the world a fairer place for both sexes!

REBECCA LURY

Rebecca's career in PR spans a decade providing strategy, policy, public affairs and communications support for clients in a range of sectors. She was shortlisted as Public Affairs Consultant of the Year in December 2014 and is currently a partner at Pagefield. Alongside her day job, she is Deputy Leader and Cabinet Member for Culture, Leisure, Equalities and Communities at Southwark Council, where she has been a Councillor since 2012 and recently stood for election at Labour MP at St Albans.

In our interview, we discussed the challenges of working in an industry that is overwhelmingly male, learning how to fight your corner, the leadership qualities in women, what women need to do to succeed, and how the 'lad' drinking culture still exists.

WHY DID YOU CHOOSE A CAREER IN PR AND PUBLIC AFFAIRS?

I studied history and politics, and I worked for my local MP while at university. A career in public affairs combined my desire to directly help achieve business priorities with my interest in politics.

I started on a graduate scheme at Edelman and spent a month in each division: technology PR, corporate communications, healthcare PR, public affairs, strategic media, digital PR and consumer PR. It was good to have the foundation of all the different disciplines.

Then the financial crash came in the middle of the grad scheme, which impacted all seven of the grads. That's when I moved into public affairs and corporate communications at Fleishman Hillard. I worked my way up to senior account manager over four-and-a-half years, working across financial services, food and retail, energy and technology and telecommunications.

I've worked in global agencies, small agencies and in-house. Every time I moved to a new place, there were new challenges and new opportunities. I love to help businesses achieve their commercial objectives – especially by combining my expertise in politics and business. I understand the complexities of politics, and it's extremely satisfying to use this to help businesses make decisions.

I love it when I'm presented with a problem I have to unpick and solve. I like to look at it from all the different perspectives.

WHAT ARE THE CHALLENGES WORKING IN PUBLIC AFFAIRS AND CORPORATE COMMUNICATIONS?

I work in an industry that is overwhelmingly male.

Often, I've been the only woman on the account team and early on in my career, I did feel that women were overlooked. For example, I discovered that one of the guys in my team, who was more junior than me, was being paid more, so I raised it with my boss. Women need to make sure they do something to address this.

I've also experienced the assumption that as a woman I'm the more junior, even though I'm a partner now. A new client, who's male, unconsciously addressed the more junior guy first, assuming he was the partner. When you bring it to their attention, they're embarrassed, of course, but it's still happening.

I'm the only girl in my family with four boys – so I learned how to fight my corner. It's important that we help women be more confident and stand up for themselves.

When I first started working, it was very much the 'lad' culture – drinking, late nights – it was hard. That hasn't substantially changed both at work and at the council.

WHAT ARE YOU MOST PROUD OF IN YOUR CAREER?

I'm immensely proud of becoming a partner. When I started out, I wanted to be an account director at 30, and I achieved that at 25, and by 30 I was a director. I've had a range of experience with different agencies and faced lots of interesting challenges and different hostile situations.

I'm proud that my work makes a real difference for my clients. My work has purpose and value. My work has given me skills to succeed on the council, and my work on the council has helped me do my job better.

I'm proud that I've garnered the trust and respect of people. It gives me confidence that I must be quite good at my job. People value my expertise.

WHAT ARE THE UNIQUE CHARACTERISTICS THAT WOMEN HAVE THAT HELP THEM SUCCEED?

Hard work – women seem to work much harder. I work until 9am to 10pm every night, which definitely impacts my work/life balance. I'm always on call.

Dependability – women will change their plans when they're really needed. They'll change their dinner plans, they'll take a call when they're on holiday. They get ahead because they make sacrifices. Guys won't sacrifice going out to watch the football.

Relationships – women are better at building relationships. They're softer, they build rapport, sometimes by just making the tea or coffee. Women talk about stuff; they share their personal lives. Men don't talk about their personal life. Talking helps women build better relationships.

Sharing – because they're in a minority, women gather together at events and share experiences and continue to learn through that.

These are all great leadership qualities.

WHAT ARE THE CHALLENGES THAT WOMEN ENCOUNTER IN PR AND PUBLIC AFFAIRS?

There really aren't enough women in the pipeline – there aren't enough women coming through. The perception is that it's a male industry – politics and media communications. It's cut-throat. There is the perception you have to be a 'go out and get it' type of person. That puts women off. Women don't think they're qualified when they look at the job description; if they only tick half the boxes, they think they can't do it. Men just go for it anyway, thinking, maybe I can do that. Women want to please; they don't want to let anyone down.

Women don't self-promote; they just get on with their job. They don't need for everyone to tell them how good they are at it.

The culture you work in is also really important. It's brilliant when you have someone who champions you and helps you out. But I've seen women who hold other women back – whether that's jealousy or fear that another woman will do the job better than them.

I think it's also still hard to find female role models in this industry. There's a lack of women. They don't want to work in an environment where they have to be 24 hours on call. It's especially difficult if women have a family. A lot of the women are just like the men; they're very competitive, they feel they have to be a match for the men.

When I was debating running for Deputy Leader of Southwark Council, I was unsure whether or not to go for it. I had this thought that I couldn't have everything. Then I thought about my choices, and I made a decision to go for it.

WHAT ARE THE CHANGES OVER TIME? FROM WHEN YOU FIRST STARTED YOUR CAREER TO PRESENT DAY.

The #MeToo movement has created awareness of the problems and the inappropriate behaviours, but it hasn't stopped it. Women are still having to work within it. Politics is the worst place for female harassment and that hasn't changed. Women are now more willing to call it out, so it may change over time, but it will be slow.

WHAT ADVICE WOULD YOU GIVE TO A WOMAN WANTING A CAREER IN PR AND PUBLIC AFFAIRS?

Women need a thick skin. They have to work with a lot of different people with different agendas.

You have to fight your corner. If you have an opinion, you should stand by it. Be quick at convincing. You need to have trust in yourself.

You have to be willing to push back; pick your battles, but pick the right ones.

It's different for men. Men are given more respect. If a man is quiet, they just say he needs to come out of his shell. If a woman if quiet, that puts her on the back foot, makes her inferior. It's unconscious bias.

At Pagefield where I am now, it's like a big family. We're in one big office and everyone cares. The senior team and the young women I work with inspire me every day. They are clever, ambitious and great fun to be around. They make work enjoyable, and I want to help them to grow as much as others have helped me. You still need to know your mind and pick your battles, but it's in a safe and supportive culture.

IT'S IMPORTANT THAT WE HELP WOMEN TO BE MORE CONFIDENT AND STAND UP FOR THEMSELVES.

– REBECCA LURY

LOTTIE UNWIN

Lottie's career in marketing was inspired by her foray into tabloid journalism. After a solid marketing foundation at P&G, she discovered her entrepreneurial spirit and helped grow the start-up, Propercorn, before a lifestyle change took her to India, a freelance career and growing her side hustle, The Copy Club community, into a business.

In the interview, we talked about a lightbulb moment coming from the shop floor, the power of generosity, kindness and building networks, embracing differences, how the quest for work/life balance is archaic, and her passion for the future of work.

HOW DID YOU GET INTO A CAREER IN MARKETING?

I started my journey in journalism at Cambridge. I studied English and worked for an online news service called *The Tab*, a tabloid proposition. We did page 3, salacious headlines, tried to be as red top tabloid and provocative as possible. I started writing, then editing.

I realized the higher up I got, the better I got. I was organizing and managing. Now, I realize, in corporate language, I was being a leader and was building a brand. There were 300 volunteer writers producing content on a weekly basis, and they were all writing in a specific way and building a coherent brand. I became business manager for a year to commercialize it. That was another penny dropping in my head – I've built a brand and this brand has engaged customers and commercial value.

I then went to Procter & Gamble for four years, where I learned brand management. I skipped to work every day – I loved it. The feedback culture and focus on real classroom training was incredible, and we had so much ownership of the work itself. The more senior I got, the more well rated I was, but the more I got moved into less entrepreneurial roles.

I realized I had that entrepreneurial spirit in me. While I loved P&G, I didn't want to stay there.

I joined Propercorn at 24 and had the culture shock of a lifetime. The first six months were the worst of my career – making that adjustment from big to small. It's like changing continents. But I grew with the business, learned a lot. We doubled revenue, won over some big retailers and got serious about digital and trade marketing. We grew up as a team.

Now, I run London's largest network for marketeers called The Copy Club. It started with me trying to make friends in similar roles to me who could help when things get tough. All the conversations I had were so energizing that I wanted to get everyone together so they could share ideas. Fast forward to today and we're a community of over 1,000 members and have two events a week for entrepreneurial marketers. For 18 months now I've been working as a head of marketing across a portfolio of small businesses and focusing on making the network an invaluable resource for our members. I absolutely love what I do.

WHAT ARE THE DEFINING MOMENTS IN YOUR CAREER?

At P&G I started as brand manager for Lacoste, the smallest brand in the fine fragrance portfolio. I changed the business model and drove 9% growth within a year, which was unheard of. I had a real lightbulb moment when I worked as a shop assistant in Debenhams, Blackpool before Christmas trying to understand what sold the product. The only reason

Lacoste was bought was because mums didn't know what to get men for Christmas and shop assistants were recommending it. I realized all that mattered was a compelling advocacy plan. I didn't need the Kantar deck to learn that. That helped me understand my skill-set and got me ready for more resource strapped smaller businesses.

My time at Propercorn shaped me hugely. I was hired as a data-driven, formally trained, traditional marketer, working with a founder who is incredibly instinctive, deeply creative and visionary – she believes overthinking is the detriment to creativity. It was a clash of two worlds. When we understood we were coming from opposite points of view, we became firm allies and counterparts with complete respect for our differences.

At Propercorn, I also learned how to manage my time. I find the work/life balance thing quite archaic. I don't want balance – I like my life, like my work and I don't care how much of each I have, so long as I'm happy.

Me going freelance was career defining. My partner got a job in India. I wanted to change my life so I could spend time there with him, and I needed a project to work on. I went to my network, told them about my big life change, what I was trying to do and asked – can you help? The response was overwhelming and gave me courage. It also gave me faith about being kind to people – I always had that ethos of helping people out. Then, when I needed to pull in favours, I was awestruck by how generous people were with their time and energy. People just asked around the office, "Has anyone got anything we can pay Lottie to do?" Before I knew it, I had loads of work, then three months later, I had a business.

That was built off kindness and karma. That was a defining moment of how I operate going forward. It's special, it works, it's good for business.

WHEN WE UNDERSTOOD WE WERE COMING FROM OPPOSITE POINTS OF VIEW, WE BECAME FIRM ALLIES AND COUNTERPARTS AS OPPOSED TO COMBATIVE.

– LOTTIE UNWIN

WHAT IS YOUR EXPERIENCE AS A WOMAN
IN MARKETING?

Marketing in small businesses is female dominated. I don't have the gender stats of The Copy Club community, but at a typical event, we will have 14 women and two men.

I've built a community by being true to my own personal values and by being warm, friendly and helpful. I find assumptions about whether those are female or male traits deeply uncomfortable.

I believe that the way we think of work will be unrecognizable in my children's lifetime, and we need to embrace a new future. I've worked between Delhi and the UK for 18 months and haven't lost a single piece of business because I can't be in the office. It requires a different approach. You must be accountable, but it makes you better at your job, not worse. I'm more productive, focussed and strategic because I'm not surrounded by day-to-day office politics.

The narrative around flexible work is wrong. We currently see it as a compromise, a second-best alternative to the way work should be, instead of embracing a more modern approach as a better way. Flexibility allows me to be inspired by things that are outside my remit. There are so many examples of things that I have brought back into UK businesses that are directly inspired by life experience in a different country. I think diversity of experience is good for business.

HAVE YOU ENCOUNTERED CHALLENGES AND BARRIERS
AS A WOMAN IN MARKETING?

Marketing can be seen as fluffy. It's not always appreciated as a core business function. I sometimes wonder if a man in a suit delivering a message to his counterpart in sales or finance is likely to be more credible than me – as power dressed as I could be.

I know there are gender differences in the workplace globally. In India, there are huge barriers for women. I worked for six months as marketing director for a large FMCG business in Mumbai and the board and senior leadership were all men. There are countless examples of gendered comments made to my Indian colleagues. There is a devastatingly huge gulf in countries like this that will never be overcome in my lifetime.

In the UK, we are more nuanced and complicated. There's a whole other paradigm – deeper questions – like whether there are genuine differences between genders. If the differences are real, how do individuals play upon them? Do I behave in ways that are gendered? If I do, how much am I ok with that? How much of that is me – and that's fine. Or how much of that is dangerous – fulfilling a stereotype I'm trying to challenge?

I heard about a girl working for a gallery here in Delhi. Her boss thought she was great because she always closed the deal – and implied she'd used the way she looked to do it. People are still hustling – and all credit to them. I don't feel comfortable with that ethically, but there's a case to say that's just human. It's naïve to think people are going to leave their sexual identity at the door when they go to work.

I don't believe that men and women are that different. I've spent my whole career being described in quite male language – maybe that's why I've been successful. If we talk about being clear in our judgment, able to empathize, good storytellers, then I don't see why women are more empathetic than men, I don't see why men are more clear than women, or whatever.

INSIGHTS & THOUGHTS ON A BRAVE NEW WORLD

THE OLD WORLD

- "We'll never allow a woman on the executive floor."
- "When they played the video back, you saw that the camera guy was more interested in focusing on my legs than my head."
- "Despite being the most profitable unit, when the promotions were announced, we were overlooked in favour of two underperforming men."
- "I'm regularly the most senior member of my team but men still often still assume I'm there to pour the coffee."
- "When I came back from maternity leave, I had to take a job that was a lower grade than the one I had when I left."

When we set out to write this book, we wanted to celebrate the huge contribution women have made to marketing, but we knew we would encounter some hair-raising tales of prejudice. We certainly did. Some made Giles' jaw drop, while Katy was less surprised. as she had experienced similar things herself.

THE TIMES ARE CHANGING

The world where quiet women were ignored and loud women may have been heard but were often ignored or, at worst, were called shrill and pushy, is changing.

In 2013, Sheryl Sandberg wrote *Lean In*, a seminal book for women in the workplace, encouraging women to sit at the table, make your partner a real partner, and don't leave before you leave. At the time of its publication, there were many positives to be taken from it regarding women's empowerment; it highlighted the biases and double standards around ambition, success and likeability, and advocated a shared earning/shared parenting style for mothers. However, it also came under a lot of criticism, not least from Michelle Obama, for encouraging women to adhere to a way of working set up by men rather than fighting for major changes in the way companies work.

Lean In opened up the conversation, but it was the 2017 #MeToo movement that gave all women the voice to speak out, for their voices to be heard, taken seriously and for action to be taken – not just against harassment, but all gender prejudices.

We're now at an exciting tipping point where the number of women in the workplace and in leadership positions is growing; women are working their way into more prominent positions, and women's networks are blossoming and creating greater impact. The collective voice of women is now emerging stronger and clearer, and it's being amplified by many enlightened men.

There is greater understanding that the problem is prejudice and unconscious bias, that the problem lies with organizations that overlook women and prevent them from contributing their skills and qualities in the workplace.

BRAND-NEW THINKING

When we set this in the context of marketing, the world of branding is changing too, and this presents a clear opportunity for women and female characteristics to play a major role.

We are facing a number of challenges including the impact of COVID-19, economic recession, climate change, and increasing political tensions, resulting in more social activism (e.g. #MeToo, Black Lives Matter, and LGBQTIA+) and consumers are wanting and expecting more from brand owners. It's brands with a strong purpose and principles that are succeeding in difficult times.

Consequently, brand thinking has been moving away from the old-world principles. Marketers no longer spend their days reducing their brand positioning to a single sentence or focusing solely on shareholder returns. Brands are finding their purpose. It's no longer just about money and success.

There's an acknowledgement that brands are more complex and need to consider their role in society, their impact on the environment and their contribution to diversity and inclusion.

Purpose is defined in an EY (Ernst & Young) report for the *Harvard Business Review* as "An aspirational reason for being that inspires and provides a call to action for an organization and its partners and stakeholders and provides benefit to local and global society." More pithily in *On Purpose: Delivering a Branded Customer Experience People Love* by Smith and Milligan, the mantra for purpose is described as "Stand up, stand out and stand firm," which translates to:

- Stand up for something: define your reason to be, an authentic and credible sense of purpose, a reason 'why' you exist beyond the desire to make profit.
- Stand out from the crowd: be distinctive, be different from what others do.
- Stand firm to your beliefs: stay true to who you are.

A result of this is that there needs to be a more holistic take on the brand that balances masculine and feminine perspectives, enabling teams to build more sustainable and successful brands for the 21st century.

It means that some of the feminine characteristics we heard about so often in our interviews should now get the prominence and respect that they are due. Many female characteristics were, in the past, undervalued or synonymous with weakness but, in the future, they are now recognized as core to marketing and leadership success. The traditional male principles of control and conquest will be tempered by kindness and collaboration.

These powerful 'feminine' characteristics focused on:

- **Empathy** – the ability to listen attentively and ask questions, understand and think about issues from someone's else's perspective, be present and focused on the person or conversation, to see people as people and not just 'consumers.' Successful marketers also apply this to their relationships with their teams, colleagues, clients and customers. Not only does it foster a kinder and more caring culture resulting in a healthier, happier and more engaged, creative marketing teams, but it also engenders a deeper understanding and respect for customers and their needs.

- **Intuition** – neuroscience has now confirmed there is nothing esoteric or magical about it. Our brain captures facts, impressions and information at lightning speed long before our intellect comes into play. Traditionally, intuition was regarded as fluffy because it was not rooted in facts and data. It was almost as if a woman's intuition had no place in the business of marketing. In today's world of data overload, being able to make an intuitive leap, then back it up with data, is a real competitive advantage. Women are constantly curious, they notice stuff, which means they are subconsciously gathering data, which is then often expressed as a 'feeling' or something that does or does not make sense. There are countless examples of these 'feelings' being proved right and resulting in sound marketing decisions.

- **Communication and collaboration** – women like to talk; they ask questions; see things from different perspectives; they encourage and promote individual development; sharing information as well as their thoughts and emotions comes more easily to them; the networks they form are open, inclusive and generous. We were struck by the modesty our Wonder Women exhibited and how often they cited their biggest sense of pride being in the teams they had built together with their strength of relationships with clients and customers. Their success in marketing wasn't about 'me,' it was about 'us,' about respecting others, unlocking potential, inspiring and empowering teams to create great brands, campaigns and innovations. One other difference many mentioned was 'volume.' Women communicate well, but the way they do it is often quieter. It isn't about how loud you can speak, but what you say when you do.

- **Staying real and grounded** – this is undoubtedly essential to being connected to your consumer/customer, but it also emerged as key to the success of our female leaders in marketing. Today's successful leaders know they are not perfect but learn from mistakes and strive for continuous improvement. All of the women we talked to were highly self-aware, constantly challenged themselves and were able to pick themselves up when things went wrong. They had learned to stay true to themselves, bring their whole selves to work and create space for others also to be their authentic selves.

Despite our labelling these as 'feminine' characteristics, none of our interviewees wanted to make sweeping generalisations about the division. They all acknowledged that there are men who possess many, even all, of these characteristics. Our Wonder Women quoted male and female role models and mentors who had exhibited these very characteristics.

What was emerging was a belief that it will be the collective voices of women and men, with a corresponding mix of 'masculine' and 'feminine' traits that will help us effect change; change that will be good for brands and business.

Many are hoping and expecting this trend to lead to a more holistic purpose-led future. It is a trend that is likely to be accelerated in a post-COVID world.

Encouragingly, there are numerous studies showing the benefits of adopting and delivering a brand purpose. There are also an increasing number of reports showing how a more gender-inclusive company culture leads to both happier employees and a healthier bottom line. The reasons for this include not just diversity of people but diversity of the types of thinking.

WOMEN AS POWERFUL CONSUMERS

If that isn't enough to help tip the balance for more equality for women in marketing, the latest research into the women's spending power will help press home the message. Women are the world's most powerful consumers, and their impact on the economy is growing every year.

Women drive 70–80% of all consumer purchasing, through a combination of their buying power and influence. As primary caregivers for children and the elderly in virtually every society in the world, women buy on behalf of the people who live in their households, as well as for extended family and friends.

The reality is that in just about every category, women are the dominant customer – maybe it's time to change the oft-quoted old adage from 'the customer is king' to 'the customer is queen' or simply retire it and focus on that other gender-neutral saying, "The customer is always right."

If women make up a significant portion of your customer base, it makes sense that they should be represented on your management team. Research shows that companies with gender-balanced teams have a higher ROI. Though things are changing, marketing like some other industries are still struggling to really shift the dial when it comes to senior management, but it is something that needs to happen.

Marketing has been, and still is, a very broad church, where women's skill-set plays strongly. Women have been well represented in PR, qualitative research, planning, brand management but they were in the past often most valued in what were seen as 'women's categories'; fmcg, beauty, cosmetics and fashion. Historically, they were less well represented in sectors like finance, alcohol, utilities, B2B, and they were underrepresented in the most senior roles.

THE PARENTING TRAP

When we asked our Wonder Women the questions, "What are the challenges women face in a career in marketing? Are these different from the challenges that men face?," there was one issue that most of them came back to – parenthood.

We frequently got into a discussion about becoming a mother and its impact on women's roles and likely future success in marketing.

It was interesting that many felt that, when a woman becomes a parent, her career was likely to plateau or go backward, but when a man becomes a parent, his career is likely to soar.

Listening to our interviewees and thinking back on our own experiences, we knew it is wrong to assume that when women become mothers, they become less committed to their work than their male colleagues, or that part-time working reduces their intellectual or professional capabilities.

As Sally Howard put it in her book *The Home Stretch*, "it's not only the glass ceiling that holds women back but the sticky floor too."

Many talented and hard-working women willingly sacrifice career progression to achieve the 'balance' they need, but more enlightened organizations are starting to do things differently. They have begun to realize that it's not a female problem, it's a problem with the way companies expect everyone to work. These organizations are moving away from the traditional male model of leaders working long hours out of home enabled by the support, not just of one woman at home looking after the family but another PA/secretary (likely to be a woman) in the workplace. They are moving to more flexible working policies, offering a range of parental support systems, and career progression that might not be linear and might take longer, but will not enforce a ceiling. And this does not just apply to women; men also need to negotiate more workable arrangements to free them up to help with parenting and household management.

Technology and flexible working hours, as exemplified in the recent COVID crisis, have further shown the potential of these new ways of working. It is something that both female and male Millennials and Gen Z are demanding, too, as they see it gives them more freedom and flexibility.

Many of our Wonder Women talked about how parenthood wasn't taking 'time out,' but that it was actually great training for leadership! For them, the benefits that being a parent bring to the workplace should not be underestimated: raised emotional intelligence, better negotiating skills (try negotiating with a toddler), increased perception, seeing things from different perspectives, clear decision making, ability to juggle multiple balls, managing and prioritizing time, delegation, creating efficiencies. This list goes on and on.

Rather like the new thinking on brands, we would argue that there is a need to change our mindset and create working environments that allow everyone, women and men, to pursue a career and raise a family at the same time. As a provocation, we wondered whether, rather than coming back at the same level or below, some women deserved to come back with an immediate promotion.

A final note on parenthood. It is also important to remember that not all women (or indeed men) want to come back full time and forward-thinking marketing departments and agencies need to see the opportunities for better part-time, flexible working and freelance roles.

THE FUTURE

Despite huge advances, gender inequality remains a fact throughout the world affecting social, political and economic life. Women are paid less, underrepresented in government and media, and often still financially dependent on men, but our Wonder Women's view of the future is a positive one.

What we loved most about our stories and interviews was the very clear message that diversity and inclusion is the way forward. It's not about advocating an all-female future;

it's not about denigrating or being in competition with men; it's about blending both male and female characteristics, creating gender-balanced teams, working together and being successful together.

We need to be aware of the differences, appreciate them and use them to our advantage. Often women and men bring different perspectives, which ultimately lead to better understanding, better problem solving, higher creativity and greater opportunities.

We need also to realize that some men are exceptionally blessed with what are still called feminine characteristics and there are some women who have the masculine characteristics in abundance.

In an ideal future where gender isn't an issue or a barrier, marketing can focus on ensuring the right balance of cognitive diversity. It won't be about what gender you are, but how you think and what you can bring to the team or leadership role that will be important.

It will be a future where not only is thinking diverse but so too are the routes to the top. Career paths are becoming less linear and more 'squiggly,' and that should mean that sideways moves and career breaks, whether for travel, further study or parenthood, are accepted and seen as beneficial.

We think the future is bright, the future is diverse, the future is inclusive.

Here's to the marketing men and women who will make it so.

Our plea to you, based on our beliefs and all we have heard is (suitably "marketing-esque" as 4 Bs):

- **Be aware** of your unconscious bias; both men and women have been conditioned with deeply engrained stereotypes – watch out for them and mind your language.

- **Be generous** in your support for women; mentor them, train them, promote them and encourage them to highlight their achievements, but don't forget men either.
- **Be open-minded** about career paths that don't fit the norm; instead, think about the benefits that squiggly careers bring. Be a champion of gender diversity and shout about how you will profit as a result.
- **Be brave** – be willing to change yourself, be willing to encourage other to change and be willing to drive change in your brand.

FURTHER READING

We don't believe your interest in this subject will start and stop with this book; ours certainly hasn't. We've therefore compiled a further reading list of books we found interesting, insightful and thought-provoking. As you will have seen, we have referenced some already. We don't necessarily agree with what all of the authors argue, but that is part of exploring a topic.

It is not an exhaustive list, and we would be delighted to hear from you if you think there are any serious omissions.

Slay in Your Lane
– Yomi Adegoke & Elizabeth Uviebinené (HarperCollins Publishers Limited)
From education, to work, to dating, to representation, money and health, this inspirational *Slay in Your Lane* explores the ways in which being black and female affects each of these areas.

Women and Power
– Mary Beard (Profile Books)
Shows how history has treated powerful women; examples range from the classical world to the modern day, from Medusa and Athena to Theresa May and Hillary Clinton.

The Strengths Book and The Strengths Workbook
– Sally Bibb (LID Publishing)
Understanding your strengths will make you fulfilled,
happy and successful, enabling you to make choices about
career and work that are right for you.

Blind Spots
– RJ Brideson (Wiley)
A provocation to the marketing world that they aren't ready
for next big $28 trillion disruption to hit the changing busi-
ness landscape: WOMEN.

The Book of Gutsy Women
– Hilary and Chelsea Clinton (Simon & Schuster)
Ensuring the rights and opportunities of women and girls
remains a big piece of the unfinished business of the 21st
century. This book celebrates the women throughout history and around the globe who have overcome the toughest
resistance imaginable to win victories that have made progress possible for all of us.

Modern Women
– Kira Cochrane (Quarto Publishing Group)
A collection of 25 pioneering women whom we can all look
up to as role models.

Invisible Women
– Caroline Criado Perez (Penguin Random House)
Uses data and stories to show us how, in a world largely
built for and by men, we are systematically ignoring half the
population, resulting in perpetual, systemic discrimination
against women.

Feminists Don't Wear Pink
– Scarlett Curtis (Penguin Random House)
A collection of writing from extraordinary women, from Hollywood actresses to teenage activists, each telling the story of their personal relationship with feminism.

The Female Lead
– Edwina Dunn (Penguin Random House)
For girls, it can be hard to identify role models in our society. This is a presentation of 60 inspirational women from many walks of life who have changed the world and are an inspiration to women everywhere.

What would Boudicca Do?
– E. Foley & B. Coates (Faber & Faber)
Entertaining stories of 50 of the most celebrated women from history whom you can turn to for advice.

Men
– Anna Ford (Corgi Books)
Goes back to the world of the 1980s to explore what men think of women and how they see themselves as lovers, husbands, fathers and sons.

Thrive
– Arianna Huffington (W. H. Allen)
Looks to redefine what it means to be successful in today's world by likening our drive for money and power to two legs of a three-legged stool. It may hold us up temporarily, but sooner or later we're going to topple over. We need a third leg – a Third Metric for defining success – in order to live a healthy, productive and meaningful life.

Nice Girls Don't Get the Corner Office
– Lois P Frankel (Business Plus)
Reveals a distinctive set of 130 behaviours that women learn in girlhood that ultimately sabotage them as adults, and how to eliminate these unconscious mistakes.

Blink
– Malcolm Gladwell (Little, Brown and Company)
Argues that intuition is not some magical property that arises unbidden from the depths of our mind. It is a product of long hours of experience and intelligent design.

Mindframes
– Wendy Gordon (Acacia Avenue International Limited)
Mindframes are models of thinking about people in relation to brands, communications, marketing initiatives and organizations. Wendy Gordon has identified six enduring principles that explain why people think the way they think, behave like they do and say what they say.

The Home Stretch
– Sally Howard (Atlantic Books)
Forty years of feminism and still women do the majority of the housework. We may be fighting for equality in the boardroom and the bedroom, but unless we also have equality in the kitchen, women will never succeed.

The Confidence Code
– Katty Kay and Clare Shipman (HarperCollins)
Combines research in genetics, gender, behaviour and cognition – with examples from successful women in politics, media and business to offer inspiration and practical advice on what women need to close the gap and achieve the careers they want and deserve.

Wifework
– Susan Maushart (Bloomsbury)
'Wifework' is shorthand for the relentless routine of husband maintenance. Husbands and wives may say they are committed to equality. Yet, whether employed or not, wives still perform an astounding share of the physical, emotional and organizational labour in marriage – everything from housework to 'sex work.'

Why Women Should Rule the World
– Dee Dee Meyers (HarperCollins)
Looks at the obstacles women must overcome and the traps they must avoid on the path to success, and imagines a not-too-distant future with more women standing tall in the top ranks of politics, business, science and academia.

Everywoman
– Jess Philips (Hutchinson)
By demanding to be heard, by dealing with imposter syndrome, by being cheerleaders, doers not sayers, creating networks and by daring to believe that women can make a difference, women can.

Work Like a Woman
– Mary Portas (Penguin Random House)
Described as "a manifesto for change," Mary Portas argues we need to move away from outdated alpha male cultures in business. The system isn't working for women, it's probably not working for many men and it's unlikely to work for Millennials and iGens.

Women vs Capitalism
– Vicky Pryce (C. Hurst & Co)
Although the #MeToo movement has empowered the mind, full power for women won't be achieved while economic inequality remains. Shows that gender equality is good for business and economics, but only government intervention can empower women.

Lean In
– Sheryl Sandberg (Penguin Random House)
Seminal book for women in the workplace, encouraging women to sit at the table, make your partner a real partner, and don't leave before you leave.

The Other Half
– Simona Scarpaleggia (LID Publishing)
Argues that inequality among human beings is one of society's biggest problems and how women's empowerment can change the world.

Equal Power
– Jo Swinson (Atlantic Books)
Power remains concentrated in the hands of men across the worlds of business, politics and culture and that's why gender inequality is so stubbornly persistent. Whether you are a teenage student, a global CEO or a taxi driver, there is much we can do as friends, consumers, parents and colleagues to create a world of equal power.

Rebel Ideas
– Matthew Syed (John Murray/Wren & Rook)
Champions the power of 'cognitive diversity' – the ability to think differently about the world around us, and how to harness our unique perspectives and pool our collective intelligence.

The Squiggly Career
– Helen Tupper and Sarah Ellis (Portfolio Penguin)
How to navigate the world of work in a way that suits you through discovering your super-strengths, addressing your own self-limiting beliefs and building your network – your own 'support solar system.'

Little Black Book
– Otegha Uwagba (4th Estate)
The essential career handbook for creative working women, it takes you through how to negotiate a pay rise, build a killer personal brand and networking like a pro.

ABOUT THE AUTHORS

Katy Mousinho is now enjoying a life of 'freedom and flexibility', having forsaken the world of full-time working to pursue multiple activities including writing, health and fitness, travel and helping out small businesses with their brand and marketing strategy.

As Managing Director of The Value Engineers and with 30 years' experience in insight and brand strategy, she's gained a broad perspective on the world of consumers and brands, having worked with a diverse range of clients across categories and countries. What she loves most is seeking inspiration from multiple sources to form insights that drive brand strategy and customer experience.

As a mother of four boys and now a grandmother, she understands the challenges of combining family life with career and is a strong advocate for getting the right support systems in place, flexibility in working patterns and being your authentic self. She is a feminist and is proud to be part of the fight for equal opportunities, recognition and rewards for everyone.

Giles Lury is a VW Beetle-driving, Lego watch-wearing, Disney-loving, Chelsea-supporting father of five who also happens to be a director of brand consultancy at The Value Engineers.

He has worked in advertising, market research, packaging design, corporate identity and, most extensively, in brand consultancy. His specialist subjects are brand positioning and innovation.

He has published three previous books of brand stories with LID Publishing, *The Prisoner and the Penguin ... and 75 other modern marketing stories* (2014), *How Coca-Cola Took Over the World ... and 100 more amazing stories about the world's greatest brands* (2017) and *Inspiring Innovation: 75 marketing tales to help you find the next big thing* (2019).

He is still amazed and slightly ashamed how few of these featured women he'd heard of previously and hopes this book goes some way to redressing that (unconscious) bias.

ACKNOWLEDGEMENTS

The first thank-you will also answer one of the questions authors are always asked – "What was the inspiration for writing the book?"

So, it's a big thank-you to Callum Lury. Callum is one of Giles' sons and a singer/songwriter who fronts The Blue Highways, an Americana band. One day, he and Giles were discussing writing. Giles asked him how he felt about writing songs from a woman's perspective and how many he had done. Later, Callum turned the tables and asked Giles, "Of all the brand stories you've had published, how many of them have a female lead protagonist?"

That led Giles to discovering how the figure was only 15% and made him decide to do something to redress the balance.

In chronological order, the next thanks should go to Paul Gaskell, CEO of The Value Engineers, who agreed to give Giles the time to work on it. This was less of an issue for Katy, who, as she says herself, has moved into a period of 'freedom and flexibility' and so could choose to commit to a project that combined one of her passions, championing equality for women, and one of her goals, to write a book.

There are also all the other people at the Value Engineers who have helped along the way and deserve acknowledgement, but Lucinda Toole deserves a special mention. She not only helped with proofreading (and Giles' writing needs it) but provided numerous very insightful observations and builds. She hopefully can see how many we incorporated.

Next, thanks to Susan Furber and Martin Liu, who agreed to publish it. Subsequently, we should of course thank the whole team at LID for all their contributions, especially Matthew Renaudin, who designed the book.

Moving on, we come to a very big and very special thank-you. It's for all our interviewees. By now you'll know who they are, but they all first agreed to participate, then gave us the time to interview them (and there is so much more we could have published from each of those interviews). They all then gave us their time and patience in finalizing their individual pieces. We cannot overemphasize how valuable we think these interviews are. They provide great insights and wonderful stories but do so in a way that allows the reader to feel that they can hear them in their own words and perhaps get to know them at least a little.

Katy and Giles would, of course, like to thank each other. It was truly a joint effort and one they both enjoyed despite, or perhaps because of, the fact that it is Katy's first book and Giles' first co-authored book. They can genuinely say that their mutual respect and friendship deepened and maybe that's the best thanks they could ask for.

Finally, Katy would like to thank her husband Gordon, and their four boys, James, John, Joe and Antony, for supporting and championing her throughout her career and on this project. Similarly, Giles would like to thank Karen, his wife and his other children including Rebecca, Giles and Karen's daughter, who we jointly thought merited her place as a Wonder Woman.